PERSEVERANCE

A Reflection of Pain, Passion and Purpose

May this book uplift, heal, encourage, and inspire!! thank you for your support!!

KING JESUS PRESS LLC

i

PERSEVERANCE

A Reflection of Pain, Passion and Purpose

A Memoir by:
SHEIRRA MARCI, Ed.D.

ISBN: (Soft cover) 978-0-9998489-6-8

ISBN: (Hard cover) 978-0-9998489-7-5

ISBN: (E-book) 978-0-9998489-8-2

Library of Congress Control Number: 2021924191

Author photo courtesy of: Telly Brown

DEDICATION

To Alijah, you are truly my reason why. You are the reason I made the decision to keep fighting. You are the reason I never gave up. When things got hard, I knew you were depending on me to keep going. Everything I do is for you. Remember, you are already equipped with the necessary tools inside of you to be successful. Remember, you can do all things through Christ who strengthen you. I love you.

To Mother, Momma K., & Daddy, words will never be enough to convey my appreciation for you all down through the years. The countless sacrifices, love, and support means more than you know. I would not be here without you.

To My late grandparents, Grandma Dean & Granddaddy Dean, I miss you both so much. I appreciate all the life lessons I learned from you both. At times, I made decisions based on what you felt I should do, instead of what was best for me. By making the biggest mistake of my life, I learned the toughest lesson. However, it made me better. I love you.

To My late Grandma Perkins, your love, support, guidance, and wisdom over the years made me a better person. You always believed in me and made me feel loved. I miss you so much. I am forever grateful to God for our time together.

To Sergio, Pachess, Shaundra, Amanda, Scott Jr., Katura, Sumarra, & Scott III, your love, support, and encouragement means so much.

v

To all my aunts, uncles, and cousins, your support means more than you will ever know.

To all my sisters, close friends, and best friends, your authentic love and support played an integral role during this journey. I pray this book touches each of you.

To women all over the world who can relate to being a single mom, juggling several jobs at one time, attending school full time, who dealt with some form of physical abuse, stability challenges, self-worth struggles, or inadequate relationships, this book is for you. May it encourage, uplift, heal, and inspire you. Remember your past does not define your future, and if God be for you, who can be against you? Never give up!

CONTENTS

FOREWORD

Life... is often like a math problem, the components of which are the result of our personal choices that fall into two categories: problems and solutions. If our choices are not a part of the solution, then they are by default just part of the problem. Faith in God and His word helps to guide our choices.

Challenges show up and need to be addressed and navigated to arrive at a set endpoint: success and happiness. Those challenges include education, careers, family, personal worth, and the distractions which often accompany them: love, children, religion, and social affiliations.

We seek validation for our choices to justify our efforts, and it helps us to press on. Time measures our growth. With time, we calculate whether we have achieved our goals. Once completed, we then testify of a job well done and a mission accomplished where God gets the glory.

This book is that testimony of success and happiness despite the challenges and distractions that inevitably come with life. It is proof that our God is able to do exceedingly, abundantly above all that we ask or think, according to the power that works in us. - Amen.

Scott W. Dean, Sr.
General Overseer, The BibleWay Temple of God, Inc.

INTRODUCTION

Perseverance is defined as being persistent in doing things despite challenges or delays in achieving goals. Perseverance serves as an act of determination which is used to obtain success. To persevere means to stay the course in the midst of difficult situations. Things in this life are not always easy. Every day will not be perfect. There will be difficult, complicated and complex times along the way. However, the way those challenges, roadblocks or setbacks are handled is vital to accomplish success.

Over the years, I endured pain. I experienced physical abuse from an individual I was forced to marry. I struggled with creating a stable home for my son. I worked two jobs at a time to ensure I could manage my household bills. I watched my son battle anger issues because he discovered the physical abuse I endured from his dad. I encountered numerous deaths in my family which impacted my mental well-being. I experienced delays and setbacks in obtaining college degrees. I got to the end of my Doctor of Education program and ran out of financial aid. I struggled with identifying my self-worth. I was involved in relationships that should have ended right after they started. Those failed relationships are preparing me for my King. They made me a better woman. It was these life lessons that prepared me to receive all the things God had planned for me.

Through the pain, I discovered my passions. I learned that tutoring kids is quite fulfilling. Being a personal assistant for two massage businesses opened the door for greater opportunities. Planning and coordinating events make me extremely happy. Nothing gives me more joy than seeing a client smile from my work. In addition to the satisfaction from my clients, these passions generate additional sources of income. I developed a sense of appreciation for the gifts God blessed me with. I use my gifts to help and inspire others to use theirs through volunteering and mentoring. I am passionate about making a difference and demonstrating random acts of kindness. As I discovered my passions, I also determined my purpose. Due to the hurt and pain endured over the years, I had a desire to get to know God for myself. I wanted a relationship that would have the greatest impact on my life. Instead of dwelling on religion, I became intentional about building a meaningful relationship with God. My love for writing is one reason for this book. Secondly, I wanted to share with the world, my sisters, my friends, and my family, that we are not defined by our past. In sharing my journey, I pray that it encourages, impacts, and inspires you to never give up. Keep going and keep fighting until you accomplish your goals. Remember, you can do all things through Christ who strengthens you. Keep pushing forward. You got this!

PERSEVERANCE

Chapter 1

HARDEST TEST

In February 2001, there was no sight of my menstrual period. It is now March, and I am feeling nervous, uneasy, and anxious. It was the first time I noticed my chest pounding. The visitor I was used to seeing every month since I was 12 years old was officially missing in action. Unsure what to do first, I went to my significant other. I explained that I missed my period for February. He immediately suggested I take a pregnancy test. Of course, I knew that was the best option, but I was extremely nervous. My heart was beating fast. I could not stop shaking. I was scared. Fear of the unknown has always had a major hold on so many. In that moment, I allowed it to take hold of me.

Nonetheless, I pulled myself together and went to the Dollar Tree to purchase a pregnancy test. I made the decision to get a test from the Dollar Tree because at that moment, a dollar was all I had. Not to mention it was close and convenient. There were so many questions running through my head when I walked in the store. I found myself, once again, shaking uncontrollably. My heart was beating faster than ever it seemed. Would the test be accurate since it was just a dollar? If it is positive, what would I do? Would I successfully carry my baby to full term? There were so many thoughts, the anxiety was building.

When I got back home from my Dollar Tree run, I took the pregnancy test and waited a short time for the results. During that time, my heart was beating faster, and there were knots in my stomach. I felt like I was going to be sick. The sweat pouring from my forehead was unusual. The bathroom was spinning. It felt like I was going to pass out. After about two minutes or so, two solid lines evidently indicated a positive result.

The adrenaline I felt in that moment was like nothing I had ever experienced before. There was no doubt in my mind the test was wrong. The fact remained; I missed my period which never happened before. The positive pregnancy test just confirmed why my period was missing.

After sharing this news with my significant other, we decided it was time to see a doctor. Within a few days, I visited the local health department. I made the decision to go to the health department because it was the most affordable and convenient option. Since I was inexperienced and 19 years old, I felt it was the best choice. It was also close to my home. My significant other had to work and could not go. I was all alone. When I arrived, I was instructed to take a second pregnancy test. It was, once again, confirmed I was in fact expecting my first child. The nurse practitioner explained that I had to have my blood drawn so they could perform a series of tests. How was I going to do this? I hate needles. My veins never seemed to cooperate. I was told my veins were small and, in some cases, they move. I did not know. What I did know was every time anyone attempted to collect blood, I had to be stuck multiple times. I hated it. I was filled with so many emotions all over again. Not only was I pregnant, but now I had to get blood drawn for everything it seemed.

Within a few days, I had to return to the doctor to obtain the results from my blood work. I soon learned those tests were precautionary measures for myself and the baby growing inside me. For the most part, I was healthy, and the baby was developing as expected at that point. Then, my doctor asked a very strange question that was offensive and shocking, "How many sexual partners do you have?" I thought to myself, "Is this a normal question, or is this something she only asks 19-year-old black females?" Without thinking twice about my response, I stated, "One. My husband." Her response was based on my test results. "You currently have chlamydia," the doctor said. Extremely annoyed, embarrassed and upset, I asked, "What does that mean?" She explained, "You must be treated to ensure it does not impact the baby, but it is too soon for you to be treated at this time." I imagine she could sense my frustration, so she provided me with my follow-up appointment for treatment and walked me out. There were so many thoughts and emotions going through my mind in that moment.

One, I was pregnant, which presented several feelings and emotions alone. Second, I had just discovered I had my very first sexually transmitted infection which could impact my baby if left untreated. Third, I had to have a discussion with my significant other and determine who he had been sleeping with besides me. I did not know much about chlamydia prior to that day. However, my doctor made sure I was well informed. After discovering that chlamydia is a sexually transmitted infection and I was only sleeping with one man, it was clear how I got it. I was truly disappointed and angry!

When I got home that evening, I had a long conversation with my significant other about what I discovered at the doctor. Understanding that I was with child, I knew I had to alleviate as much stress as possible. I made it clear he needed to be treated and I would not consider intimacy with him without protection again. I was not sure if this was something he had before me or since being with me. Either way, I was no longer interested in being intimate with him. I was confused, but most importantly, I was hurt. My number one priority was protecting the baby. After a few days passed, I was finally in a place mentally where I could share the pregnancy news with my family and friends. The news of my pregnancy was received well by most. There was a lot of love and support for me and the bundle of joy on the way. It was refreshing and put my mind at ease. However, there was still a nervous energy I was dealing with.

Even though my immediate family was supportive of my pregnancy, I knew it would be different delivering this news to my grandparents. The one thought that nagged me was, I was not married! Yes, I told the nosey doctor I was already married without thinking twice. The truth was I was not married yet. This was a big deal. Having children out of wedlock was frowned upon. I was taught no sex before marriage. Since I am from a very religious family, I knew better. "For unto whomsoever much is given, of him shall be much required" Luke 12:48 KJV I knew my family would not receive it well. After some time had passed, I went to my grandmother while in church, and told her I was pregnant. As I think about it, I do not remember anything else about the conversation except, "Getting married is the best option, you must get married." Those were her exact words. I was extremely overwhelmed with the thought of getting married. I had so many questions but could not process the words fast enough to ask. I wondered, "What would be the benefits of getting married?"

It soon became clear why getting married was the best option per my grandmother. Getting married meant I would not lose the positions I held in the church, which included choir member, usher, and Women Fellowship co-secretary. In addition, it meant I would not have to make the dreaded apology in front of the entire congregation. Whenever women got pregnant out of wedlock, they were required to apologize in front of the whole church. It was very humiliating.

At that point, getting married made sense. I did not want to let my family down. I felt compelled to get married based on the conversation with my grandmother when she made it clear, "You must get married." When I got home, I spoke to my significant other about marriage. Since getting married was not a topic we previously discussed, it was pretty awkward. I provided a brief overview of the conversation I had with my grandmother. I explained my beliefs and why this was a big deal in the eyes of my family. I told him we should do what was right. I convinced myself that getting married was the right thing to do in the sight of God. At the end of our discussion, we came to a mutual agreement that we should get married. Even though we both agreed to get married, I spent the next several days wrestling with myself. Is this really the best option? Is my significant other really someone I wanted to spend the rest of my life with? Why is this so difficult? In the end, getting married was the best option. Not because I was in love or could not imagine life without my significant other. It was simply because I felt forced to do so. A small part of me felt like this was something God wanted me to do, but I was not sure. I never prayed about the decision. I never talked to God about what I should do, and I learned that is a mistake most of us make. We listen to man instead of listening and obeying God. Since my grandmother was very passionate about marriage and felt it was the best choice, I never considered anything else. After several red flags, physical abuse, and fighting for my life, I still made the decision to get married. This was the hardest decision I had to make.

In May 2001, the day arrived when I finally said, "I do." On Wednesday, October 24, 2001, at 7:26 a.m., I gave birth to a beautiful baby boy, Alijah Sherrod Granville. From the first moment I laid eyes on him, I knew my life would never be the same. I was a mother. I was responsible for an entire human being. It was surreal. By the grace of God, labor and delivery went well. The journey to motherhood commenced. After years of fighting for my life, Alijah's life, and being physically abused, I made the decision that enough was enough. In March 2003, badly battered with a busted blood vessel in my eye, I walked away from my marriage and never looked back. After the decision was made to get married for the sake of my family, I made the decision to do something for me. No one was more important in my life at that moment than Alijah. I vowed to protect him and keep him safe which meant I had to make tough decisions. Although, I was officially done with my marriage for obvious reasons, I provided several opportunities for Alijah's dad to be a part of his life. However, he made decisions that excluded being there for Alijah. We learned to adjust through it all.

As a single mom to a one-year-old male child, I knew God was the only one who would see me through this challenging time in my life. As one of the hardest tests, it was clear making the decision to get married because I got pregnant was not the right decision to make. I dealt with the decision until February 12, 2009, when my divorce was finalized. Since divorce and remarrying is frowned upon in my family, I kept the decision to file for a divorce to myself. Besides, divorce was not something I ever imagined, but I needed to officially conclude that chapter in my life.

I am grateful for this test because it made me stronger. God protected me through it all. Sometimes the tests we go through are meant to help us grow through them. I never thought I would be in a situation where I had to fight for my life or my son's life. However, I learned to make necessary adjustments to ensure I did not experience that again. Physical or verbal abuse is not okay. Get out. Get help. Walk away before it is too late. I got to a point where I had to not only think about my life, but the life of Alijah as well. Since I vowed to protect him, I did what was necessary to keep him protected. He deserved a loving and peaceful home. I made sure he had that by any means necessary.

Chapter 1 Lesson

Verbal or physical abuse is never okay. It is not healthy and should not be accepted under any circumstances. Get help, get out, and never look back.

Chapter 2

STABILITY TEST

After the separation from my husband, it was clear I was now a single mom with a full plate. I was extremely scared and overwhelmed with how I would make it through this time. However, I moved forward realizing that God had never left me nor forsaken me, and He would not start now. I was working at Cato as a full-time manager. I was the 1st assistant store manager with major roles and responsibilities to fulfill each day. I was truly grateful for the income, but it was not enough for all my household bills. Now solely responsible for rent, lights, gas, car note, car insurance, and childcare, things were rough for me. I had no help from Alijah's dad and no additional resources. I was drowning.

By the end of 2003, I was working two to three jobs, but eventually had to move in with a family member. My aunt let me live with her until I got back on my feet. Living with her was ideal because it was very close to my job. Not only did my aunt let me live with her for a little while, two of my close female cousins allowed me to live in their homes as well. Though I was truly grateful for these options, I knew I wanted to be in my own place with my son.

After moving from place to place, I moved back home with my parents in Stone Mountain, Georgia. Unable to afford regular childcare while I worked, I started letting one of my older cousins babysit Alijah during the day. She was the cousin old enough to be my mother, because she had a daughter older than me. She always had a house full of kids. The kids enjoyed being at her home because there was plenty to eat, lots of toys, and several movies to watch. In addition, she always took them to different places like the mall, movies, park, and fun attractions. I was grateful to finally have reliable childcare at an affordable price. Since I was always working, my cousin and I agreed it was best to let Alijah stay with her during the week and pick him up on the weekends. Most times I was working on the weekends as well, so I did not see Alijah much. I was missing him. I knew I needed to make some major changes fast.

After two years of healing and rebuilding from a battered marriage, I took a chance on love again. In April 2005, I met a guy while we were both renting cars at Enterprise. Not sure how things would develop between us, I questioned whether or not I was ready. It had only been two years since I officially separated from my husband. The physical abuse I encountered was just two years prior. Though I vowed to never let that happen again, exploring a new relationship too soon could create more damage to a very delicate situation. Taking these things into consideration, I still took a chance.

Things started well with this new man in my life. I met his kids and family. After several months passed, I finally introduced him to Alijah. Things were going so well, I eventually moved in with him. I did not allow Alijah to move in with us. He was still with my cousin during the week while I worked. However, on my off days or early days, I had Alijah with me.

In May 2007, my life shifted again. My significant other was arrested. In addition, the Department of Family & Children Services for Douglas County had Alijah in their custody. I was at work when things went down at home. Very worried and concerned about losing my child to the system, I left work immediately to determine what was happening at home. My heart was racing. I was shaking as I drove through traffic from Marietta to Lithia Springs. Once again, I was overwhelmed with emotions. I was unsure of what was happening at home. I knew I needed to get there immediately to get to Alijah. He mattered more than anything else. I did not want to lose him.

Upon arrival, I was ordered by the police to provide access to a home that technically was not in my name. I was bullied and threaten. I was told if I did not provide written consent to enter the home, I would lose my son. Alijah was standing on top of a police car screaming, "Momma." My attempts to get to him was blocked by a police officer who was adamant about me providing consent to enter the home. Extremely livid, I asked, "What is going on? Why is it so important to grant access to a home that is technically not mine?"

Since I had no idea who was in the home, I did not know what to do. Was it our roommate they were looking for or was it my significant other? The police shared with me there was a potential suspect in the home who was being accused of burglary in the apartment complex. I was shocked. I was worried. I was still trying to process it all. Then it became obvious that the individual they were calling a suspect was, in fact, my significant other. I was numb and confused. After several protests and extreme frustration, I signed the consent giving them access to the home. Immediately upon receipt of my signature, the officers and dog went into the place I once called home.

The scene was unfamiliar. I had never experienced this before. After a short time passed, I heard the dog barking and the officers yelling. I was officially scared. I was trembling as I stood there thinking what would happen next. Within a few moments, the officers, dog, and my significant other were coming from the home. It was at that moment I realized my once stable home was starting to crumble again. I could no longer ignore the knots that were in my stomach. Before I could breathe a sigh of relief, I was ordered by the officer to follow him in my vehicle to the police station. Considering they were still in possession of Alijah, I knew I needed to do whatever they asked to get my son back.

When we arrived at the police station, there was a caseworker onsite to watch Alijah. Without thinking I asked, "Why are you taking him? Where are you taking him?" I did not understand why he was not being returned to me. I was informed I needed to answer more questions. What questions could I possibly answer? I was at work. The officers were very vague in the details surrounding the case. I was very puzzled. All I wanted to do was get my son and go home. Little did I know, Alijah would not be going home with me that day. After several calls to different family members, the case worker confirmed my father was on the way to get Alijah. I was so relieved they were releasing him to family versus state custody. I had a few days to prove to the caseworker that Alijah would be living in a stable home and receiving adequate childcare. It was clear, returning to the apartment my significant other and I occupied was not an option. I was provided an option to stay with his mother instead. After the home was inspected by the caseworker, Alijah was released back to my custody. I was grateful, appreciative and relieved to have my son again. I realized things could have been a lot worse.

Determined to never put myself or my son in that position again, I worked hard, saved money, and moved back into my own place in August 2009. The same cousin who kept Alijah while I worked during the week, got an apartment in her name for me. It was the fresh start I needed to ensure my son and I remained in a stable environment. Within just a few short months of on time rent payments, I was able to put the lease in my name. It took longer than expected. However, I was finally in a place where I consistently provided a stable home for Alijah and me. From 2009 until now, my son has not experienced any stability challenges. He was no longer bounced around from home to home. I still let Alijah visit family on the weekends, but he had to come home on Sunday night. I was determined to do everything I could to ensure Alijah was safe.

Having a stable home is so valuable when raising a child. As a mother, it was my responsibility to provide a stable and loving home for him. Sometimes, it took working two to three jobs at one time. Other times, I had to make countless sacrifices. Most importantly, I had to take accountability and stop relying on others to provide a home for me and my son. I am truly grateful for the lessons learned. Once I tackled my stability test, it was time to conquer the next task at hand.

Chapter 2 Lesson

It is not how you start, but how you finish. Remember, change is necessary for growth. Do not be afraid to grow. Do not be afraid to ask for help. Do not hold on to your mistakes. Release it and let it go.

Chapter 3

EDUCATIONAL TEST

In 1999, I graduated from Redan High School in Stone Mountain, Georgia. With an overall high school GPA of 3.2, I was automatically considered a HOPE recipient. The HOPE Scholarship is a merit-based award available to Georgia residents who demonstrated academic achievement during high school. I was extremely grateful this scholarship was available to me to help cover the cost of college. However, I knew it would take more than money to get into college. I recognized very early I was not a good test taker. However, my grades were high enough to attend community college. I was extremely disappointed when I was not accepted into Georgia Southern due to my SAT scores. This was another challenge I faced, but I did not let it stop me.

After being accepted into Georgia Perimeter College - now a division of Georgia State University - I scheduled the Compass placement exam. The scores from the Compass exam determined what level math and English courses I would take. After scoring very high on English, there was no doubt I would take college level English courses on day one. I did not have the same success with math. To avoid taking learning support math courses, I needed a score of 32. I scored 30. I was very discouraged. I realized this was just another test I would eventually get through. To pass the learning support math class, I had to obtain a "C" or higher and pass the exit exam. It was such an excessive process, but

I moved forward, nonetheless. I passed the class two semesters straight but could not master the exit exam. Math was never my best subject. Often anxious with the different concepts needed to solve problems, I never liked math. On the third attempt, I was only allowed to take the learning support math class. I knew this would delay me finishing my degree, but there was absolutely nothing I could do about it. Half-way through the semester, I was told the required score needed to pass the Compass exam changed. Instead of needing a score of 32, the required score was now 30. My instructor told me at this point all I needed to do was pass the class. Though highly disappointed, I was relieved the class was almost over. My aggravation came from the fact that when I initially took the test, I made the required score needed to avoid taking a learning support math class. I quickly learned this would be the first of many challenges on my educational journey.

After about two full years at Georgia Perimeter, I learned a tough lesson that was not taught in high school. Unbeknownst to me, I learned withdrawing from classes each semester impacted my financial aid eligibility. One morning before heading to class, I went by the financial aid office. The hold on my account from the business office prompted my visit. After speaking with the financial aid representative, I was perplexed. I was informed I no longer was eligible for financial aid. The reason why I lost financial aid was because more classes were attempted than completed. That meant any time I registered for a class, attended the class for several weeks, and dropped it at mid-point, it impacted my completion rate. I was never provided this information which made me feel worse. I stood there shocked, annoyed, hurt, and in disbelief. It took a moment for me to gather my thoughts. After a few moments, I asked, "What does this mean?" The representative spoke the dreaded truth, "If you plan to remain in school, you must pay for classes out of pocket." I immediately turned around and walked away. Before leaving campus for the day, I went to the business office to officially withdraw from all my classes. The sad truth was I could not afford to pay for school out of pocket. I felt sad, disappointed, and defeated. I had no idea what to do next, but I knew I would not throw away my desire to further my education.

From 2003-2009, I made no attempts to return to school. I had several thoughts about returning, but it never seemed like the right time. In addition, I had no idea where to start. It was always my goal to obtain a college degree. Therefore, I knew it was time to face my fears and do what was necessary to return to school. In July 2010, seven years after losing my financial aid, I started the process for returning to school. Since having resources to pay for school was vital, I applied for financial aid first. By the grace of God, I was eligible again. I was overwhelmed with joy, happiness, and gratitude. Being eligible for financial aid meant I could resume my educational journey. Second, I applied to another community college. This time, I was accepted into Atlanta Metropolitan State College. It was a smooth transition. I learned what not to do from attending Georgia Perimeter. Therefore, I was in a much better space this time around. Third, I was intentional about seeking support when it was needed and conducting research when I was unsure or when something did not make sense. In addition, I partnered with classmates to ensure I had reliable individuals to study with. This support served me well.

In May 2013, I graduated from Atlanta Metropolitan State College with an Associates of Art degree in English. My grandmother was extremely proud. Her exact words were "I do not know what took you so long, but I am glad you got done." I told her I was not done yet. One of her final words to me before she passed away was, "Don't stop. Keep going." Due to my own personal goals and her words, I was determined to keep going and not stop. After being accepted into Kennesaw State University, I started my next degree in June 2013. Even though my grandmother passed away five months later in November, I still remembered her words, "Don't stop. Keep going."

I was devastated when my grandmother passed. Heartbroken, sad, and in a dark place, I needed to reset to make it through such a difficult time. I wanted to stop. I wanted to give up. I was in such a low place. Losing a loved one is truly hard. Especially someone who has played an integral role in your life since you were born. After a few days of being in a dark and low place, I quickly realized she would not be happy about me thinking about leaving school. Therefore, after a brief leave from my classes, I pulled myself together so I could finish the semester strong.

In December 2014, I graduated with my Bachelor of Arts degree in English. An accomplishment worth celebrating, I planned, coordinated, hosted and funded my very own graduation party. I enjoy planning events. Especially those that are my own. I put a lot of thought and consideration into the location, invitations, theme, colors, food, guest list, and personalized party favors that I made by hand. The day of the event, I had more texts and calls from those who would not make it versus those who would come and help me celebrate. Very hurt, I considered calling everything off. However, that meant I would lose a lot of money I had already invested in making this event one to remember. I was not interested in allowing money to go to waste, so I continued with my graduation party as planned. Though extremely disappointed by the lack of support, I was quickly reminded those who were supposed to be there for me, were there. If one of my best friends, Lashawn could fly into town to celebrate with me, my family and friends living in Atlanta had no excuse. It was a beautiful event nonetheless, and I was extremely grateful for the memories made.

Little did everyone know, my journey was not yet complete. My overall goal was to become an English professor, so I realized I had to keep going. In March 2013, when I lost my job in retail, I started my tutoring business - *Marci's English Essentials.* The first year I started tutoring I had 10 children. I was truly grateful for the opportunity. I love my students. They all had a unique story that I could personally relate to. It was truly a blessing and such a humbling experience for me. The parents trusted me to help their child improve in several subjects. When they received progress reports or report cards, there were always improvements. The parents were so impressed, I soon became highly recommended to other parents who wanted to take advantage of my services. In addition to event planning, I discovered another purpose in my life - tutoring. It was the referrals from my parents that kept me busy over the years. I count it all joy. I have tutored individuals of all ages starting at age 4-33. I assisted several college students with papers and major projects. Though I have no classroom experience, I have no doubt in my abilities to be an effective English professor when the time comes. It is my passion.

This passion has caused me to keep moving forward. In January 2015, I was met with several challenges on my quest to start graduate school. To attend grad school, I had to take the Graduate Record Examination (GRE). As I previously mentioned, I am not a good test taker. I used test prep material provided by my childhood best friend, Shakia. She was also preparing to attend grad school. It was so encouraging having someone to study with and embark on this journey together. She was very encouraging through it all. Not only did she provide study material, but she suggested additional resources such as websites, flash cards, and practice tests. With the resources provided, I studied as much as I could.

Despite all the efforts, the scores I obtained were not sufficient. I was denied enrollment to Kennesaw State University's Master of Writing Program. I was very discouraged. I wondered why a school I recently graduated from with over a 3.0 GPA would make the GRE a requirement for admission. If my grades, writing samples, and entrance essay were exceptional, a test should not be the determining factor.

Even though I did not agree with this process, I was still determined. For the next several days, I researched and reached out to my resources to determine all available options. I could not be defeated. I would not be defeated. After doing research on different schools, I discovered most traditional colleges and universities required a certain score on the GRE to be accepted. Therefore, I explored options that did not have the GRE requirement. After speaking with admission advisors from the University of Phoenix and Strayer University, I finally made a decision. I decided to attend Strayer University where I enrolled in the Master of Education program with a specialization in Adult Development & Training. The program was exclusively online which worked well with my home-work balance. It truly takes discipline to be successful in an online program. With papers due every week, I had to create a schedule that would ensure my success. From July 2015 to September 2017, I worked hard on my master's degree. I submitted all assignments on time or before time. I communicated regularly with my instructors and addressed any concerns as soon as they occurred. In addition, I was engaged with my classmates in the virtual course room which was beneficial when I needed a study partner.

On September 23, 2017, I graduated with my Master of Education (MEd) degree with an overall GPA of 4.0. I was extremely proud of my efforts and hard work. To complete such a rigorous program with all A's was truly commendable. I was grateful. Upon completion of my master's degree, I realized I was one step closer to the finish line. Within only two weeks of finishing my master's program, I was enrolled in my final program, Doctor of Education with a specialization in Adult Education. Everything started well. It was basically a continuation of my master's program. Even though the classes were similar, I was in an advanced program on a higher level.

In July 2019, I realized I was reaching the maximum allowed for federal student loans. Again, I was met with a new challenge. The thought of running out of financial aid had not crossed my mind. I was stressed. I was worried. I asked myself, "Did I get this far not to finish?" I spent days trying to figure out how I would pay for my final classes. I was quickly reminded that God did not bring me this far to leave me. If he brought me to it, he would bring me through it.

One day, I was talking to my boss and business partner, Errol, about my challenges with school. He never liked to see anyone stressed or worried about anything. He was always supportive and encouraging. This time was no different. When I started explaining what was going on with school, he simply asked, "What do you need and when do you need it by?" After providing all necessary details, he made it clear I no longer had to stress about it. When it was time to pay for my courses, for two quarters, he covered it for me. I was extremely grateful and appreciative of the gesture. In May 2020, I completed my final requirements for my Doctor of Education program. I celebrated with a photo shoot which included Alijah because he was graduating from high school. It was such an exciting time for us both. In June 2020, my degree was conferred, and my educational journal was officially complete. Due to COVID-19, all in person graduation ceremonies were canceled. Though extremely devastated, I was grateful I was able to participate in a virtual ceremony on

September 17, 2020. I know if my grandmother were here, she would be extremely proud of my perseverance. I pushed through until the very end. There were several roadblocks along the way, but God was faithful through it all. As a result, I am now Dr. Sheirra Marci, and no one can take that away from me.

Chapter 3 Lesson

When you feel like giving up, remember why you started, and commit to finishing strong no matter what. Sometimes, it will get hard, but keep going. You got this!

PERSEVERANCE

Chapter 4

SELF-WORTH TEST

As a young girl living with my mother, things were not always easy, but I learned to adjust. As much as I can remember, even with her drug addiction, my mother did what she could to take care of my sister and me. We had clothes and shoes for school. Most times for dinner we had enough food to eat. Even when the refrigerator was empty, she made a way to feed us. I have fond memories living with my mother. There were also challenging ones. Nonetheless, I never recalled seeing my mother fighting a man or being physically abused by one. Yet, that became my reality with my first relationship as an adult.

Charming, smooth, and obviously a lady's man, Alijah's dad was different. His approach was different. The words he used to talk to me were different. The way he treated me initially was different. In my mind, this was a special different. We met one day while we were both at work. Being a full-time manager for Cato was not for the faint at heart. It was very busy and demanding. This was my first job, so I wanted to do a great job. Plus, I was referred to the company by a church member. I did not want to make her look bad. I also wanted to prove to myself and others that I deserved to be there.

After six short months of being a store associate, I was promoted to second assistant manager. Due to the stress of the job, it was important to step away and take those much-needed breaks. I was on lunch break, so I decided to walk up the sidewalk to Kroger. As I walked along the sidewalk I was greeted with "Hello Ms. Cato." I looked around trying to determine who he was talking to. Not realizing clearly, it was me as I was the only one wearing a Cato name tag. Since I do not like attention, I was instantly mad at myself. However, I said hello. To avoid what was coming next, I kept walking. It did not matter, because as it turned out he worked for Kroger. He continued to talk to me.

At some point in our encounter, we exchanged numbers. I got what I needed from the store and went back to work. I learned a lot about him in such a short time, but it was not enough. After multiple phone conversations, meetings at work, outings around the city, we met at his home. I quickly learned he did not have his own place. He was sharing his current home with his oldest sister and her kids. His sister was about her business. She was extremely protective of her family and people coming into her home. Needless to say, she wanted to know who I was and where I came from all of a sudden. Once we talked, she was very friendly and happy to meet me. Things were going really well between us. We spent a lot of time together. Sometimes we went out to spend time together. Other times we stayed inside and watched movies. No matter what we decided to do, we always had a great time. He treated me the way I thought I was supposed to be treated as a young woman.

August 2000 is when he and I met. In February 2001, just six months after meeting, we got an apartment together. I was 19 years old and officially in my own place with a man who I truly thought loved me. We selected an apartment that would be convenient for us to get back and forth to work since we did not have a car. Things were good, and then it happened. After being with his father all day, he came home drunk and angry. Who was this person in front of me? I had never seen this side of him. What caused this shift in behavior? Why was he so mean? Does drinking alcohol really cause people to be violent? I still do not recall what the issue was, but I clearly remember the first slap. I held my face in disbelief that he actually hit me. He started accusing me of talking to other men or being with someone else. I had no idea where all of this was coming from. If I was not at work or school, I was at home. I was so confused and bothered that I was being accused of something I was not doing.

After the first encounter, I convinced myself it would not happen again. The sad truth is it continued. A few weeks later, we found out I was pregnant. With the news of being pregnant, I assumed the abuse would end. Who could physically abuse their partner who's pregnant? Why endanger the unborn child or future mom by subjecting her to abuse? I was still so young so I did not understand how someone could do that to anyone, especially myself. Another day with his father and he returned home mean as ever. I could not figure out the root cause of all this anger. What was he dealing with while with his father that caused him to come home and take his frustration out on me?

I remember trying to convince him not to spend so much time with his father because it was impacting our relationship. However, he took that as me trying to tell him what to do. "You're trying to control me and stop me from being a man," he would say often. It was pointless trying to convince him I was trying to help our relationship. I remember saying, "If something is impacting our home, why not do what is necessary to eliminate the problem?" Nothing I said or suggested made sense to him. For that reason, the abuse continued.

One night after I got in from church, he was not home. Shortly after I started winding down, he walked in the door intoxicated again. Nonetheless, I greeted him like I always do. Not sure at what point things went wrong, but I remember running out the door. Scared, tired, upset, and confused - I was running for my life and the safety of my unborn child. I did not know where to go or what to do. To get away quickly, I left my phone in the house. I had no way to contact my family for help. "Why was I still dealing with this? I do not deserve this. Why am I allowing this person who is supposed to be my partner to cause me or our unborn child harm?" I thought. There were so many feelings and emotions going through my head. I wanted to cry but the tears would not fall. I wanted to scream, but the words would not leave my mouth. All I could do was run until I got tired then figure out what to do next.

When I got to the top of the hill in our apartment community, there was a security guard at the gate. He saw me almost immediately and wanted to know why I was outside so late with no shoes on. I tried to explain but he could tell I was very upset. While trying to explain what was happening, my partner walked up the hill. The security guard closed and locked the doors to prevent him from getting to me. He was enraged. He screamed,

"So you're messing with this dude?" He started pulling on the door in hopes of gaining access. The security guard told him to leave before he called the police. It did not matter. He attempted several times to get to me. Thankfully, he was not successful. I do not know what would have happened if he gained access. He eventually left. He walked out of the apartment community and did not return.

After some time had passed, I walked back to our apartment. I was still very worried because I did not know if he would return. If he did return, what would happen? God gave me peace long enough to fall asleep. He never returned home that night or in the morning before I left for work. I was truly relieved.

One night after spending time with my parents, he thought he saw an unfamiliar car dropping me off. Once again, he went into a jealous rage and insisted I tell him who "he was." I could not understand why he was so jealous. I had never cheated on him. I did not talk to other men. Yet, I was always being accused of cheating. He was filled with his own insecurities which caused him to lash out at me. At this point, I was angry. He asked me several times who dropped me off. I told him several times my father and stepmom, but that was not enough. He accused me of lying. Since I was trying to get Alijah ready for bed, I completely ignored the barrage of questions he hurled at me. Alijah was laying on our bed while I was changing his diaper.

Without warning, he charged at me and pushed me into our bedroom window. He pushed me so hard the window cracked. If I was a little heavier, I might have fallen out of the window. Officially scared for my life, I wrapped Alijah up in his blanket, grabbed my phone, and ran out the apartment. This time I did not hesitate to call my parents to explain what happened. They came right back to get us. Our safety was their #1 concern. We stayed with them for several days. I was torn between whether I was going back to the apartment or staying home with my parents. Of course, he called to offer apologies that I had heard several times before. None of it mattered to me in that moment. I was upset. However, I eventually went back. Why did I go back? Was I worried about what my family would say? Yes, because we were married. The suggestion to get married when I discovered I was pregnant with Alijah was why I was dealing with this foolishness. Not wanting to apologize in front of my church was the reason I was dealing with this abuse. Still being young, inexperienced, and unaware of my true value, I accepted the abuse much longer than I should. When would this end? When would I get tired? What would I do if he tried to cause harm to Alijah? It was in that moment, I realized things needed to change.

In March 2003, I finally had enough. I realized my life and the life of my child was more important than this marriage. After coming home from work one afternoon, I experienced my last and worse attack. Alijah was still very young and unsure of what was going on. I remember him being in his room playing. I was not home an hour yet before the chaos started. To get away and avoid being attacked, I fell in the hallway. When I fell, I landed on my back. He instantly climbed on top of me and started punching me in my face. One punch, two punch, three punch, four punch, five punch, six punch. I was screaming and kicking, but he would not stop. I was worried Alijah would come out his room and he would hurt him, so I tried to refrain from making too much noise. I tried to fight back as much as possible, but it did not help. He punched me so many times in my face that I felt the structure of my face change. I knew something was wrong, so I cried out again for him to get off me.

He finally did. I jumped up quickly and walked into the kitchen. I paced back and forth trying to determine what to do to protect myself. I knew with the latest attack there was no way he would let me out the house without a fight. I knew even if I made it outside, I had to come back for my baby who was still in his room playing. What was I going to do? Confused, afraid, hurt, and frustrated, I snatched all the knives from the drawer and ran out the door. I was trying to hurry down the stairs as fast as I could that I lost my balance. In addition to my already beaten and battered body, I slid down the stairs landing on the concrete where my arms, knees, and legs were scraped from the fall. As I finally screamed for help, he ran outside, jumped in the car, and drove away. At that point, I ran back in the house to get Alijah. I called the police and my parents.

While I waited for the police to arrive, I went to the bathroom and looked at my face. The image in the mirror was something from a horror movie. Battered, bruised, and blue, I started crying again. What would my parents say this time? What would they do? What would the police do? As the tears continued to roll down my face, I realized I had to pull myself together for my son. A few moments later there was a knock on the door. My father had arrived. He did not say much when he saw me initially. I explained what happened by recapping the worse attack of my life. A few moments later, the police arrived. They took my statement and asked multiple questions which included if I knew where he went. I explained to them what happened and that I did not know where he went when he left in my car. The police offered to call the paramedics. I declined. However, I did agree to go to the hospital to have my injuries examined. When I arrived, there was not much of a wait which was surprising. Once the doctor examined my injuries, he confirmed I had a busted blood vessel in my eye from the continuous punches. I was told it was nothing I could do to speed up the healing. It was evident it would take some time. Embarrassed, broken, bruised, and battered, I then had to wear dark sunglasses to cover my bruises and scars. The bruises and scars were from someone who said he loved me. I did not deserve this.

By now, several members of my family were aware of the abuse I had endured. Humiliated and ashamed, I kept my distance for a while. After spending several days with my family, Alijah and I went home. When we arrived, my car was back but the tag was missing. When we went inside, all of his things were gone. He was gone as well. For the first time in two years, I let out a sigh of relief. He was gone and I was happy. It was time to rebuild and restore. After speaking to Grandma Dean, she shared with me some things she discussed with my father. She said, "Sheirra, your daddy is really upset about you being jumped on. He said the police better find him before he does." In that moment, I realized it was time to officially let go. I was not willing to lose my father for attempting to fight this battle his way. I could not imagine him being sent to prison for causing harm to someone who hurt me. It was not worth it. The police did find him before my father did. He was arrested and ordered to stay away from me. I knew in my heart he would never be back. I was done.

When I got to a place where I could speak to him again, I let him know I would never keep him from seeing his son. I told him any time he wanted to spend time with Alijah, he could do so. The sad reality was he would not do right. Between losing jobs and going in and out of jail, the quality time with Alijah never came. Still broken from the pain, I quickly started rebuilding my life as a single mom. My top priority was Alijah.

For two years, I did not explore the possibility of a new relationship. Often, we jump from one relationship to the next when we are still broken. I did not want to repeat the same cycle over again. I needed time to heal and grow as a young woman. Being involved with an abusive man for almost two years was a sign of low self-esteem. It took some time to rebuild from the hurt and pain. Even though I was never in an abusive relationship again, I struggled with identifying my self-worth. I found myself entertaining a relationship without a title for several years. When the conversation came up about being in a committed relationship, the response was, "I am just not ready." Today, that simply means stop wasting time and move on. Back then, it meant he will eventually change, and I must be patient. This was truly a moment of weakness. It was clear I had not tapped into my true value.

In 2015, I was finally in a happy and healthy relationship. However, effective communication was a challenge. Therefore, after two years together, we broke up. One thing that I slowly came to realize was life is too short and time is too precious to waste. After years of failed relationships, I decided it was time to focus on me. I needed to find my peace and figure out what made Sheirra happy.

In November 2017, I had my very first full body massage. I had no idea what I was missing by not getting regular massages. The first experience caused me to incorporate massages into my monthly routine. I started working out consistently and being mindful of my food intake. Since happiness starts from within, I knew being happy physically, spiritually and emotionally was vital. I truly evolved during this time. I was no longer afraid of being alone. I enjoyed being alone and learning more about myself. I learned that coloring relaxes me. I learned that working out at the park was more fulfilling than working out inside a gym. I learned it was necessary to say "no" and set limits. I learned traveling and going to the movies alone was not as bad as others made it seem. I no longer cared what others thought. I was finally living for me.

I learned to appreciate each day that God blesses me with because none of them are promised. I learned to pray more and give God more of my time. I learned to truly take time to heal and not rush things. I learned to stop expecting something different, still taking the same approach. When new guys showed interest, I was intentional about making it known what I wanted and needed from the beginning. I was done wasting time that I could not get back. When the things I wanted and needed became a challenge, I quickly walked away. I was officially in a space where I realized my true value. I finally had a clear understanding of my self-worth. Things that I accepted five years ago are no longer acceptable, under no circumstances. I understand I am not perfect. I still have some things to learn. However, significant progress was made, and I cannot go backwards. I am grateful for the life lessons and the experiences. Not only have life lessons taught me well, but they also prepared me for the love of my heart. My self-worth test has not been easy, but I am a much better version of me because of my journey.

Chapter 4 Lesson

No matter how much you go through, your past does not define your future. Remember to treat yourself the way others should treat you. It starts with you.

PERSEVERANCE

Chapter 5

RELATIONSHIP TEST

In July 2019, I was preparing to deactivate my Facebook page to focus on school. Disconnecting from social media prior to the start of each quarter was common for me. I learned early there are many distractions that can impact your progress in school. I was not going to let social media be one of those distractions. Therefore, a few days before a new quarter started, I completely disconnected from social media. It may seem a bit excessive, but I did what was best for me. Usually, I made an announcement. I wanted my family and friends to be aware of why I was not on Facebook. However, most of my family and friends knew this was a common routine for me. They knew exactly where to find me if they needed me.

Summer quarter 2019 was no different, especially since my doctorate program was very demanding. On July 5, I received a random friend request from DE, a person I had never seen or heard of before. Considering we only had four mutual friends, I wondered: how did he find me? Who is he? What did he see that caused him to want to be friends with me? Was he interested in getting to know me as a person or just crushing on my pictures? I was definitely curious to figure out who DE was.

Before accepting the friend request, I reviewed his profile. I discovered he was from Buffalo, New York, his birthday was five days before mine on June 1, and he was extremely attractive. Normally, I never accept friend requests from individuals who do not have at least 50 mutual friends (which means I know them from high school), family members, and/or co-workers. In this case, I was willing to make an exception. I honestly had no idea why he was an exception to the rule. I knew I would soon find out. After pondering a little while longer, I accepted the friend request. I thought as soon as I accepted the friend request, he would send me a message via messenger which was very common. Every time I accepted a friend request from a guy, moments later he wants to know if I am single. I never understood why this is so common. Then again, it is social media which means anything is possible.

In this case, DE did not reach out to me immediately. A few hours after I accepted DE's friend request, I started seeing his previous posts in my news feed. Not thinking much about it, I reacted to the posts like normal with a like or love reaction. Later that evening I noticed a message in my inbox. Since I did not have Messenger downloaded on any of my devices, I could not view the message. The next morning when I got to work, I logged into Facebook from my desktop. To my surprise it was my newest Facebook friend DE, telling me to "Be careful." I was not sure what that meant, so I responded, "I am not sure what you mean, can you explain?" I waited for a response but did not get one as quickly as I thought. When the response did not come, I reached out again to explain I would be deactivating my Facebook page. He did not like that idea at all. Explaining my reason for disconnecting from social media softened the blow a little bit, but DE still did not like it.

Initially, I did not know if it was because he really wanted to talk to me or if he just wanted to see my pictures. My pictures seemed to attract a lot of attention. I love taking pictures. Over the years, I developed a deeper appreciation for capturing and cherishing each moment. Therefore, I take pictures almost every day. In addition, I decided to have at least one photo shoot every year to highlight a special event in my life. Of course, to thank, support, and promote the photographer's work, I share my images on Facebook. However, if my page is not active, that means no one can see those pictures.

As the day moved on, DE and I had some very deep and meaningful conversations. I started to feel like he was not only interested in my pictures, but he wanted to get to know me as a person as well. The more we talked and communicated with one another, the more it felt like DE and I had known each other for years. We had just started talking, yet it felt like he was a part of my life from a different lifetime. Within the first 24-48 hours of us connecting on Facebook, we had already talked about family members, likes, dislikes, memories from our childhood, current career roles, future endeavors, and past relationships. He made it known early that he had never been in love. He shared his challenges with relationships, and I shared mine. He admitted he was not perfect. I acknowledged my flaws too. We were very open, transparent, and honest with one another. I loved that we could talk about anything. We connected so well.

These things drew me closer to him. It was refreshing getting to know him. We had similar interests and values. We had common goals and passions. We both had a spiritual relationship with God which was vital. Our interactions were interesting, and things flowed naturally between us. He asked very important questions which included, had I ever been in love, did I want any more kids, or if I wanted to get married? I provided open and honest answers. We talked about so much that I was not ready for it to end. I was officially curious to see just how far these conversations would go.

Since things were going so well, I decided I would give him my number so we could talk outside of Facebook. He expressed his gratitude for me giving him my number. A few days later, I disconnected from Facebook to focus on school. I thought the deep conversations we had via messenger would continue. However, they quickly came to an end. I was so focused on finishing the final classes of my doctorate program that I did not put much thought into it. Communication was very minimal. We rarely spoke on the phone. When we did communicate, it was limited to texting. Within a short time, all communication ceased. In December 2019 when I reactivated my page on Facebook, I noticed we were still friends. I instantly wondered why the communication stopped if he was truly interested in getting to know me.

A few days before Christmas, I sent well wishes via Messenger. To my surprise, he responded and asked me to be a part of his new year. I was not sure if he meant it since we had not spoken since July, so I asked for clarity. My question to him was, "How do I be a part of your new year, if we are not consistently communicating with one another?" In that moment, he explained to me that due to several deaths in his family, he was in a dark place.

I could truly relate to multiple deaths in the family because I experienced something similar in 2017. Every month from October 2017 to February 2018, I lost a loved one or someone very close in my immediate circle. It was tough. It was so hard for me that I started seeing a therapist. I felt this would help me process the grief. Any type of loss is hard, especially multiple deaths within days, weeks, or months a part. I truly empathized with DE. I was very concerned about what he was dealing with. He explained the losses caused him to disconnect from social media for a while as well. However, he reassured me he was doing much better. One of the most important qualities that I look for in a relationship is an individual who is stable mentally and emotionally. Dealing with multiple losses can really impact mental health. I was truly concerned about DE and wanted to make sure he was truly in a better space.

DE and I picked up right where we left off back in July. It was exciting being able to reconnect with him. Not to mention, I was able to learn more about him as time moved on. In January 2020, we decided it was officially time to meet in person. After my company's anniversary party, we met, got food, and just talked. He opened up a little more about his upbringing, and I shared new things about myself. We connected so well. Our chemistry was authentic, and things did not feel forced between us. We had such an amazing time together. It was clear, we were both interested in dating. We wanted to see just how far things would go between us. Unfortunately, constant communication was such a challenge for DE. I was in a space where I needed strong and consistent communication. I was unwavering in that. There were certain things I was willing to compromise and sacrifice, but communication was not one of them. In an attempt to express my need for strong communication via text, he did not receive it well. When I suggested we have a verbal conversation so I could clarify my intentions, he never provided that opportunity. For this reason, we stopped communicating with one another all over again. Disappointed and highly annoyed, I moved forward knowing I tried to offer a clear explanation but was never given the opportunity to do so.

Communication is vital in any relationship. whether it is a professional or personal relationship, there must be effective communication. When two people are getting to know one another, it is impossible to do so without consistent communication. I strongly believed there was something special about DE, but he was not making it easy for me to find out. After a few sporadic text messages, all communication officially ended by mid-January 2020. Since I was not on Facebook, I was not tempted to reach out to him, and he did not contact me.

After some time had passed, I started to think about him. I wondered how he was doing and honestly hoped he was doing well. We were officially in the middle of a pandemic and life as we knew it had changed. We were under a shelter in place order which meant we had to stay home. We could leave for essential things, but we had to be home by a certain time. Yes, we had a curfew. All major companies, including my employer, had transitioned the entire workforce to an exclusive work from home platform. It was something I had never experienced before. I was truly concerned about my family, but I was concerned about DE as well. I honestly did not know why he crossed my mind so much. We had not talked to one another in months. When he crossed my mind, I would pray that he was well, and I would move forward.

In May 2020, I had finally come to the end of my educational journey. I received all approvals from the School of Education and was officially registered for graduation. It was an amazing feeling to be at the finish line. Not only was I preparing for graduation, but my son was graduating from high school as well. It was such a memorable moment in my life. I reactivated my Facebook page again on May 7, 2020. I had developed a habit of checking to see if DE and I were still friends. Considering we did not end on great terms in January, I knew anything was possible. I honestly thought he blocked and removed me as his friend. However, I learned that was not the case at all. I quickly discovered he and I were still Facebook friends. Even though I reactivated my page on May 7, I did not like or love any posts from DE. I did not text or send any messages via Messenger. I was honestly waiting for the right time to communicate with him.

On May 16' my son and I completed a graduation photo shoot with one of my favorite photographers. To recognize, support, and promote his work, I created my very first post since I returned to Facebook several days prior. The next day on May 17, 2020, I finally reached out to DE. I felt it was necessary to apologize for the misunderstanding we had back in January. It is always my goal to convey my intentions and feelings clearly. Therefore, I felt it was the right time to do so. I made it clear that I meant no malicious intent in my explanation of how much I needed communication. In addition, I let him know I did not want there to be any ill feelings toward us and I hoped he was doing well. When I sent the message, I was unsure if he would even respond. I knew I simply wanted him to know I was sorry, and I hoped we could at least be cordial with one another.

I sent the message and logged off Facebook. Within a few hours, I received a message from him. He simply said he missed me. I was relieved that he responded at all, but I was not expecting that type of response. As I pondered my response, I had to admit that I missed him too. He had crossed my mind several times in the past. Even though he was missed, I just did not think it was the right time to reach out. I was finally in a place where I wanted to communicate with him. I wanted to check on him to see how he was doing. Most importantly, I wanted to know if he was remaining healthy and safe in the middle of a pandemic. Before I knew it, we were in a deep conversation like we had never stopped talking to one another. I was a bit concerned that we would start communicating all over again and it would end shortly after. I knew I did not want this to become a continuous cycle where we talked for a few days and then it stopped abruptly. I explained to him the importance of communication. I let him know I was fine with us just being friends if communication was still a challenge for him. We both made it known that we were still interested in one another. We decided we wanted to try again to see just how far things would go. We also agreed that we would not let each other go this time. I was not convinced, but I was willing to take things one day at a time.

After several hours of constant communication, he asked if he could see me. He also asked if he could have a kiss. Kissing DE was one of the most memorable moments that I held on to from January. He was gentle, yet passionate which meant a lot to me. I was extremely excited to see him because it had been four months since we spent any time together. We planned to see each other the same day we reconnected, but time got away from us. I was a little worried because I did not want us to start on a high note and things go downhill again. I did not want promises to be made, but not kept. I was guarded. One thing for sure, I did not want to get hurt. It was necessary to protect my heart at all costs.

Considering I had not seen him since our first meeting, I was really missing him. I was open to any and every opportunity to be in his presence. I wondered just how serious he was about spending time with me. I strongly believe we make time for those things we want to make time for. Therefore, based on his actions, I knew it would prove if he wanted to see me or not. Even though I did not get a chance to see him as expected, his actions confirmed he really wanted to see me. The next day he called and texted me. In addition, he video called me which is something he had never done in the past. Actually, for the next several days, he was in constant communication with me. The same consistent communication I asked for in January but did not receive, he was executing it willingly. I was extremely grateful for the small progress we were making.

Within the next few days, we finally met in person and spent some much-needed time together. It was always difficult leaving him. It was something about simply being in his presence that made me feel safe. He was attentive. He was gentle. He was caring. He was respectful. He catered to me. He was kind. He was passionate. He was a great listener. He was all the things I needed in a man. He was truly different, but finally in a good way.

Communication between us was very strong and I appreciated that. I was no longer restricted to just messages via Messenger or text messages. We had verbal conversations and video calls. I appreciated his efforts. I wanted him to know they did not go unnoticed. I was learning a lot more about him and he was getting to know a lot about me. We quickly discovered we had similar goals. We both wanted to get married, have kids, build our businesses, and travel. He expressed several times that I demonstrated qualities that he wanted in a wife. He possessed qualities that I needed in a husband. DE and I were becoming very close. However, with our work schedules we were not seeing each other as much. I was starting to miss him a lot. He always reassured me we would spend time together soon. Even though we did, it was never enough.

DE and I lived in the same state, but it felt like I was in a long-distance relationship. It was frustrating. He lived on the eastside of Atlanta. I lived on the westside of Atlanta. We both had reliable vehicles so spending time together should not have been a challenge, but the truth is it was. I was at a place in my life where I wanted no part in anything that resembled a long-distance relationship. All relationships take work, but long-distance relationships required more work. I wanted no part in a long-distance relationship at all.

One morning, he reached out to ask if we were going to get married someday. I was not sure where that question came from suddenly, but I responded by saying yes. Even though we were experiencing a challenge with spending sufficient time together, I felt in my heart he could be the one to enhance my happiness forever. I explained to him that I was quite invested in us, and I looked forward to spending forever with him. DE let me know the reason for his question. He started the morning with a conversation about me with his oldest sister. Considering his sister plays a major role in his life, I knew this was a big deal. After DE and I reconnected, I started telling my family about him. I gave him the nickname "Mr. Forever." Everyone in my circle already knew about him. To learn he was talking about me to his sister meant he was really thinking about the future. He could no longer hide his feelings for me. I was intentional about expressing my feelings for him. Things were consistently going well for us. The consistency of it all really made the difference. I knew he was afraid of falling in love. Especially since he had never been in love before. The fact that DE had never been in love, I knew this was going to be difficult to overcome. However, I was up for the challenge. I felt deep in my heart, it was only a matter of time.

Things were going pretty good between us. Then our relationship was tested. In July 2020 as we prepared to celebrate one year of knowing one another, a female decided it was necessary to make false accusations. I sent a message to DE acknowledging a ring I purchased with our initials. I ordered the ring at the end of May, but it did not arrive until our anniversary which was July 6th. The ring was not meant to represent an engagement or promise ring. It was simply a ring that I wanted, so I purchased it.

When I sent the message to DE, I wanted to make sure he received it. Therefore, I sent it to both numbers I had for him. Within a few brief moments, DE called. He wanted to know why I sent a message to his secondary phone. While I attempted to explain that I sent the message to both phones, he mentioned it was a business phone so other individuals besides himself could see those messages. I was not sure what that meant, but I soon learned the phone belonged to his business partner at the time. He and I had a very brief conversation. Then, he told me he would call me back. Unsure why my text was such a problem, I brushed it off and continued with my day.

When I hung up with him, I started receiving text messages from the business phone. The first response was, "You ordered your own ring? Shouldn't the man give you one?" Before I could collect my thoughts to respond, I received a follow-up message which said, "This is DF. DE and I have been dating for five months. Happy Anniversary." Before I could send a message back, DE called me a second time. When I told him about the messages that were sent to me, he asked where I was. When I told him I was at home, he told me, "Do not move," and hung up. I was not sure what to do. I was preparing to leave so I could run errands. Therefore, I went to the garage and was sitting in my car.

About five minutes later, DE walked around the corner into my garage. I was surprised he was there. He asked where my phone was, so I handed him my personal phone. I was still sitting in the car trying to figure out what was going on. After a few minutes passed, I got out the car, and he followed me into the house. He went to the living room. I went the dining room. I was clueless as to what prompted the visit. I was still unsure of what was going on. Since I have two phones, I used my business phone to handle other matters while DE was still in possession of my personal phone. I waited until he said something.

Suddenly I heard him say, "Answer this phone." Finally, it was clear he was waiting for someone to return his call. I did not know who that person was, but I soon found out. Within about 10 minutes, his phone rang. He immediately placed the phone on speaker. His response was, "Man, what is wrong with you? I will not allow you to do anything to impact my home." Before he could continue a female voice responded, "You know I have always had feelings for you. It goes beyond business, and I cannot shake these feelings." He responded, "That has nothing to do with me. We only have a business relationship. If that is a problem for you, we should explore other options, because I will not let you mess up my home." The last response I heard before I walked upstairs was, "I know I owe someone an apology, and I will apologize."

At that point, I heard everything I needed to hear. As soon as I walked upstairs, he was right behind me. I explained to him that I could not entertain that energy. The individual who sent the messages was lying about her and DE dating. She felt it was necessary to introduce herself, expecting a different outcome. When DE was leaving, I told him I was preparing to respond back to the message. He said to me, "I am the King and I fight those battles for you. If we are out and anyone gets wrong with you, it is my job to handle it, not you." He made it crystal clear that I did not have to fight those battles. I had a deeper level of respect for him at that point. In many cases, men allow women to fight battles with other women. That should never be the case, but it is a sad reality. When a man is truly serious about a woman, he should do whatever is necessary to ensure female counterparts stay in their place. I had no doubt in my mind DE was serious about me. He was not interested in allowing anyone to impact what we were building together. That warmed my heart in so many ways. From that day forward, I had no other issues with any females.

DE proved to be trustworthy. He was forthcoming with information. I did not have to second guess his intentions. He remained open and honest. Even though he was very transparent, I found myself asking him not to hurt me. DE and I moved past that situation. We were stronger. We were growing as a couple. Things were going well for a while. However, there was always a test that came to make us stronger. It can either make us or break us. With our busy work schedules, we were not spending a lot of time together. I was very mindful that we both had a lot going on during the day. Sometimes we both had 12-hour days. Not to mention we lived on two different sides of town. Getting to me was often a challenge and vice versa. Days, weeks, and even a month passed, and I did not see him. I did not like it, and I expressed it every chance I could. Once again it felt like I was in a long-distance relationship, which made me extremely annoyed. I was upset. My frustrations were growing. DE reassured me we would spend time together, but we did not.

When we did spend time together, it was very limited which created more frustration. In August 2020, his grandmother who reared him was admitted to the hospital. Not wanting him to go back to that dark space he was in before, I felt it was necessary to support him in any capacity during that time. He reached out to let me know he was going home to check on her. Ironically, I was off work for a few days, so I decided to fly to Buffalo, New York as well. In that moment, I felt it was important to be with him. I attempted to communicate with him in several different ways that I would be flying to Buffalo. However, I just could not reach him. Even though I could not reach him, I still decided to go.

Upon arrival in Buffalo, I picked up my rental car and checked into my hotel. I texted DE again to let him know I was there if he needed me. In addition to letting him know I was there, I sent him my location. DE was a bit confused by my text, so I told him to call me when he got a chance. Within a short time, he called me. I told him once again I was in Buffalo. He still did not believe me. He told me he would call me back, so I went to sleep. I was extremely tired since I had been awake since 3:30 a.m. and traveling since 6 a.m.

When I woke up, I ordered food, and watched TV. Since I did not know much about Buffalo, I stayed in my room for the rest of the night. I watched movies until I fell asleep again. Around 5 a.m., I woke up to several missed calls from DE. I have a habit of leaving my ringers off, so I would not be disturbed when I am resting. I did not expect to wake up to several missed calls. Before I could call him back, he called me again. This time I answered because I was holding the phone in my hand when he called. When I answered the phone, he asked what room I was in. When I told him, he said he was on the way up.

I was filled with so much excitement when there was a knock on the door. When I looked through the peep hole, it was him on the other side of the door. When I opened the door, he was just as excited. I remember him saying repeatedly, "I cannot believe my baby is here in Buffalo." In that moment, I just wanted him to know I was there to support him in any way I could. We talked for a little while. Then we both fell asleep. I had an appointment at 9 a.m., so I had to get up in such a short time. It was quite alright because I was with DE and that made everything better.

After limited hours of sleep, I headed out to my appointment while DE got some much-needed rest. When I got back to the hotel, we started our day. We ran a few errands, met friends and family, got something to eat, and went to the hospital to visit his grandmother. With COVID-19, the hospital had very strict guidelines. Since I was not a family member, I could not visit her, but I understood. My purpose for being there was simply to be a source of support for DE. I wanted him to know I was there for him if he needed me.

The trip to Buffalo was quite refreshing. I enjoyed the warm welcome from everyone I met. DE was amazing. He made me feel safe. He made sure I had everything I wanted and needed. My time in Buffalo came to an end quickly. It was time for me to return to Atlanta, but I was not ready to leave. I was leaving a piece of my heart there which made my departure difficult. DE was not scheduled to return to Atlanta for a few more days. He wanted to spend more time with his grandmother. I understood. We said our good-byes and I was headed back to Atlanta.

After a few more days in Buffalo, DE returned to Atlanta. I was so excited to have him close again. I was also grateful that his grandmother was getting better. Within just a few short days of us being back in Atlanta together, we were preparing to leave again. I traveled every weekend in September 2020. I traveled to Nashville, Tennessee for my baby brother's wedding. I traveled to Baltimore, Maryland for a weekend with my best friend. In addition, I spent time with my uncle in Orlando, Florida. Yes, we were in the middle of a pandemic. However, I realized we only have one life to live, so we must make each day count. I took necessary precautions to keep myself and my loved one safe. DE was doing a lot of traveling as well. When we spent time together, we agreed it was time for us to take a trip together. Although we did not get the opportunity to travel before 2020 ended, I was encouraged that we would travel together soon.

As a new year began, I was hopeful about my future with DE. We continued to learn a lot about one another. We had good, bad, happy, sad, frustrating, and difficult times together. On those days when I was frustrated because I could not see him, he knew the right words to say. He always knew what to do to ensure I felt better. The main problem was work kept us both really busy. I knew we had to find a healthy balance so we would make it as a couple.

In February 2021, after a brief period of uncertainty, there was a major shift in our relationship. We began to talk more which meant our communication was stronger than ever. Our communication was no longer restricted to just text communication. We had verbal conversations which allowed us to effectively convey our thoughts to one another. We started spending more time together, inside, and outside of the home. Our date nights were truly fulfilling. Creating time to eat, hang out, and just talk was always refreshing. DE treated me well. He was so gentle, kind, caring, and authentic. He made his intentions clear and showed me the upmost respect.

When DE talked about the future, he always mentioned things like "we" and "us." He made it crystal clear he wanted me in his future. In addition, DE expressed how he felt more. Some days, he called me just to tell me he loved me. He poured into me so much positivity and I poured it right back. When he discussed his vision, he was so passionate. His drive, motivation and focus were admirable. Before long, I had fallen deeper. He captured my heart in so many ways. I often wondered if he fell for me the way I had fallen for him.

DE and I have made significant progress since we met in 2019. God has been faithful through it all. He leads us and guides us which is necessary. Only God knows what the future holds. I can honestly say God blessed me with a man who I am truly grateful to have in my life. I realize every day will not be perfect or easy. However, when God blesses you with someone who is worth the work, that makes the difference. DE is worth the work. I love him. He loves me. We both love God. With him as the head of our lives, we have a solid foundation.

Chapter 5 Lesson

Some relationships are only meant to last for a season. Some relationships last a lifetime. Be sure to identity which relationships are worth developing into something beautiful. Being blessed with someone "worth the work" means the individual is not perfect but has proven to be someone you are willing to grow with.

PERSEVERANCE

Chapter 6

MOTHERHOOD TEST

Alijah Sherrod Granville, my son shine, my pride, and joy. The one who helped shape me into a better person. In 2001, when I became a mother, I did not have all the answers. I was scared, nervous, and unsure of what to expect in my new role. Still inexperienced at 20 years old, I knew I had to figure things out quickly. Dealing with physical abuse was not a good way to start my motherhood journey. Having to fight for my life and keep Alijah protected was a big challenge. However, God never left me. He gave me strength when I was weak. After the abuse that led me to the emergency room, I did what I needed to do to ensure we were both safe. I walked away and never looked back. Even though I struggled with stability for years, I was finally able to conquer this challenge. Being in a stable home was still not enough for a single mom of a male child. Alijah deserved to be in a stable and loving home with both parents. However, things do not always go as planned or even as expected. It was in these moments I had to learn to adjust.

When Alijah was old enough to attend school, he was always referred to as sweet, kind, caring, and very talkative. That was my Lijah. It was hard for him to remain focused during class because he wanted to play and talk to his friends. He was the only child. There were no other kids at home with us. Alijah being talkative in class became a problem. I started receiving calls from teachers telling me how great Alijah was, but he talked at the wrong time. I was grateful for the relationships I developed with the teachers early. They knew they could call me at any time, and I would support them in any way I could. The school administrators and staff knew me well. I was labeled as the "Mom who meant business." I wanted them to understand if they needed me for any reason, I would be there. Alijah was well-behaved most days. Then he had those days when he did things without thinking which caused serious problems for him. Overall, there were no major issues at school. Alijah always told his teachers and friends that I was his role model. Whenever he had major projects to do or papers to write, he would often write about how I inspired him. It was such a humbling and heartfelt moment. Most kids want to be like athletes or music artists, but my child wanted to be like me. I was grateful.

Even though there were no major issues with Alijah at school, I started experiencing things with him at home. Things I had a hard time understanding. By the time Alijah turned 14 years old, he started rebelling. I think this is the period where kids start smelling themselves. Alijah was really testing my patience.

One night, I was upstairs in my room sleeping when I heard the back door open. I laid in the bed for a few minutes trying to determine if someone was trying to break in or if someone was leaving out. It was the latter. As soon as I got enough energy to walk downstairs, the back door opened again. Alijah was walking back in the door. He was not expecting me to be downstairs. Annoyed and frustrated I asked, "What are you doing outside this time of morning?" It was 2 a.m. His response was, "Mom, I was taking out some trash." What trash was he taking out at 2 in the morning? My blood was boiling at that point because nothing he was saying made sense. I told him to go upstairs and go to bed. We both went back upstairs and went to sleep.

A few days later, the doorbell rang. I answered the door and was greeted by a teenage girl from the neighborhood, "Can Alijah come outside?" I responded, "No, Alijah is busy right now." She responded, "Can he come out later?" I said, "No sweetie, it will be dark soon." Her final response was, "Alijah be outside all the time late at night." Since Alijah was standing right behind me during this exchange, his response was, "Mom, no I am not." Considering I caught him coming back into the house at 2 in the morning just a few days prior, I was starting to think there was some truth to what the girl was saying. I soon found out that Alijah was sneaking out the house at night while I was sleeping. When I asked him why he was sneaking out, his response was to hang out with his friends. His excuse for sneaking out at night was because I did not let him go outside during the daytime. None of it made sense. I explained to Alijah that anything could happen to him while he was sneaking outside. The fact remained I was in the house sleeping. If something happened to him, I would not know.

Alijah became more rebellious, and my frustrations grew each day. We started bumping heads and tensions between us grew. I could not understand what he was going through. He continued to test my patience and my frustrations intensified. I started to question my parenting. The truth is, I was a single woman trying to raise a male child. A male presence had not been in the home since my separation in 2003.

Therefore, I knew this was something he was lacking. Regardless of the lack of male presence in our home, that was no excuse for Alijah to act out in this way.

I had my father, brothers, and close male friends serving as mentors for Alijah. Sometimes the talks would help, and often, it did not. Since Alijah felt like I never allowed him to do things, I gave him an opportunity to do things he wanted to do. I allowed him to play football from 6th - 8th grade. I supported him through it all and attended every game. I was an active Team Mom for two years. That meant I was responsible for snacks, first aid, and anything else the players and coaches needed. I was Alijah's #1 Fan. I was so proud of him. I encouraged him to keep trying even when things did not go the way he felt they should.

When Alijah went to high school, I allowed him to be a part of the marching band. Not only did I support him, but I was an active part of the marching band serving as a chaperone. I attended practices when my work schedule allowed. I attended every game, band booster meetings, performances, band festivals, exhibitions, competitions, and all out of town trips. I participated in fundraisers often. The things that fundraisers did not cover, I paid out of pocket. Band fees was $400 alone. Not to mention all the performances the band had scheduled out of town. Each school year, I paid over $1,000 in fees associated with the band, in addition to maintaining our household and making sure Alijah had everything else he needed. I found value in investing in Alijah's extracurricular activities because he was staying out of trouble.

Even though my son was staying out of trouble, he was dealing with things internally that I was not aware of immediately. I wondered why he would storm off, slam the door, or punch the wall when he got upset with me. I started noticing this behavior and discovered he was dealing with a lot of built-up anger. I did not know why he had so much anger built up inside. Therefore, I asked. Alijah told me he was upset and embarrassed because he did not have two parents in the home like his friends.

He also shared with me he knew I was physically abused by his dad. This news took me by surprised because Alijah was too young to know what was happening during that time. Most times, Alijah was in his room and out of sight. Plus, most of the abuse I endured was while I was pregnant and right after Alijah was born. Obviously, someone told him. I do not think the individual who told him meant any malice, but it was truly damaging and caused stress for Alijah. He had a hard time understanding how or why anyone would cause me harm.

In addition to being angry, he was hurt. As a mother, I did what I felt was best. I scheduled an appointment with a therapist. I felt Alijah needed someone other than myself to talk to. I believed if Alijah had someone he could confide in outside of family, it would help him process and deal with the pain. Soon after appointments started, they quickly ended. There were numerous scheduling conflicts with school, work, and the therapist availability. After two attempted sessions, the option to see a therapist was no longer conducive to our schedules. Therefore, the anger challenges remained. When Alijah did not understand or agree with a decision I made, he became extremely upset. As a mother, I did not expect temper tantrums from a teenager.

One evening I came home looking for Alijah. I called out to him when I arrived, but there was no response. He was not downstairs, so I checked upstairs. After checking his room and the guest room, Alijah was nowhere to be found. I attempted to open the door to his bathroom, but it was locked. I knocked on the door several times, but there was no answer. I put my ear to the door to determine if I could hear anything, but it was extremely quiet, so I was not sure. The locked bathroom door was not an instant indicator that he was in the bathroom. Alijah had locked himself out his bathroom several time before. Therefore, I assumed this time was no different.

After several hours had past, I became worried. Alijah knew no matter how old he was, I did not tolerate him being outside when I was not home. He did not have a phone I could call to confirm where he was. I went in his room to determine if there were any clues to his where abouts. No luck. I went outside and looked around to see if I saw him. No Alijah. I went back in the house and called friends. I honestly did not know what to do. I got home around 4:30 p.m. It was now after 8 p.m. There was still no sign or sound from Alijah. I was worried, but also annoyed. I was worried because hours had passed, and I did not know where Alijah was. I was annoyed because the bathroom door was still locked, and I was not sure if he was inside hurt or what.

Frustrated with the situation, I called the police. Living in Cobb County, Georgia, it would never be just one police car arriving. They always arrived in record numbers. That night was no different. Upon their arrival, I gave them the details of what happened when I got home from work. Then, the officers asked a series of questions, "When was the last time you saw him? What was he wearing? Does he have a history of this type of behavior? Do you think he is in danger? Do you think he would cause harm to himself?" After I was done with their interrogation, they followed me upstairs. I told them I suspected that Alijah may be in the bathroom, but I was not 100 percent sure. I explained no sound or movement had come from the bathroom in hours. After a moment of being in my home, they asked if they could bust down the door, if necessary, to get inside. I explained that I was renting and could not consent to allowing them to damage the door. Thankfully, the officers did not have to damage the door to get inside. After knocks on the door and calling Alijah's name, he finally came out of the bathroom. Relieved and annoyed I walked into my room.

As soon as he walked out, two officers took him to his room to talk. Two more followed behind me to provide me with options. I was told I could file an incident report for disorderly conduct. He would have been required to go before a judge. Alijah going before the judge meant he would receive some form of punishment. Though he would not be formerly charged, which meant it would not go on his background, there would be a record for this incident. Was this the best option? Was this the only option? What would it help? Would it cause more harm than good? How does this process work?

Why would a mother file a report against her son that would essentially impact him in a negative way? After spending several minutes talking with the police officers, I decided the option provided was not a good option. As the officers started to leave, I recall one of them saying to Alijah, "You have a great mom who was worried about you. Treat her right." With those words, the officers left. There were no more police encounters with Alijah.

However, we continued to have challenges. Alijah got to a point where he wanted to work. My father never allowed my sister and I to work until we were out of high school and grown. Even then, our purpose for working after high school was to pay for college. We were still living at home, so we did not have any bills we needed to pay. Letting Alijah work was something I considered because it would help cover his expenses that I was paying for. Alijah did not know how to fill out a job application. Neither did he know how to properly answer questions during an interview. I took time to teach him how he should answer questions in hopes of obtaining a job.

With my help, Alijah got his first job at Six Flags Over Georgia. He was offered a position on the spot. I was very proud, and it was such an exciting time for him. Alijah got paid weekly. Since he was also in school, he was only allowed to work on the weekends until the summer. The first few checks Alijah received were very small, so I did not keep track of what he was doing with his money. After a few weeks went by, I started noticing packages arriving in the mail. Shirts, shorts, shoes, and hats. Alijah was spending $400 on shoes, $95 on shorts or pants, and $60 on shirts. I could not understand what would cause him to spend excessively. I took my son to Wells Fargo to open a checking account. Instead of him receiving a paper check each week, I felt direct deposit was best. This would also allow me to track his earnings with his spending.

Alijah continued to spend excessively. However, he was now required to send $200 to me each pay period to be placed into the savings account. For a little while, this was not a problem. Then, Alijah grew frustrated with having to give me anything. He felt it was suitable to pay $400 for shoes and spend money on clothes, hats, and anything else he wanted to buy, yet pay nothing toward his band fees or any other expenses. He believed since I was previously covering these fees, I should continue to do so. We both learned a tough lesson regarding the first job. After some time had passed, I told Alijah he had to put in a two-week notice. Without much fight, he submitted his request, and his last day at Six Flags came to an end. I shared with Alijah things would be different the next time around. He would have a clear understanding of my expectations, or he would not be able to work.

Alijah's high school journey was rapidly coming to an end. He expressed an interest in driving. I had mixed emotions about Alijah learning to drive due to his performance in school. One morning after meeting with his guidance counselor, I discovered Alijah did not have the necessary math credits to graduate. His counselor indicated he had to take two math classes his senior year and pass to graduate with his class. This crushed my heart. I knew math was a major challenge for Alijah. Even with weekly tutoring, it did not seem to be enough. I was proactive in speaking with his teachers and getting additional resources to assist Alijah. Failure was not an option. He did not get this far not to finish high school. Therefore, getting him through high school became my #1 focus.

When Alijah mentioned wanting to learn to drive again, I simply brushed it off. He completed his first semester of his senior year with A's and B's. One of the best semesters of his entire high school journey. The second semester presented a few challenges for everyone. The world was dealing with a global pandemic and students had to adjust to virtual learning exclusively from home. Prom was canceled. Senior trips were canceled. Senior activities were canceled. Graduation was canceled. It was a hard pill to swallow. However, I did not lose focus on what Alijah needed to graduate.

By April 2020, Alijah had officially completed all requirements for graduation. I was very proud of him. He completed his last semester of high school with A's and B's again. He did what I knew he could do since 9th grade. Once again, I was very proud of Alijah's progress and getting through his final year of high school. Things were not always easy between us, but I did what I felt was best for Alijah. I loved, supported, and protected him through it all. After a few short weeks of finishing his final assignments as a high school student, Alijah was accepted in Albany State University. I was extremely grateful and humbled by his success. One thing I have learned on this journey is being a mother is a lifetime job. With almost 20 years in this role, I know I still have a lot to learn. However, I am encouraged that God will never leave me, or forsake me. He will continue to lead and guide me on my motherhood journey.

Chapter 6 Lesson

Becoming a mother is such a lifechanging experience. Through it all, we must do whatever it takes to offer the highest level of love and support to our children. On this journey through motherhood, it is so necessary to focus on the things that truly matter. If it does not matter, do not dwell on it. Do not let anyone make you feel bad for the shortcomings. Only God can judge you.

PERSEVERANCE

Chapter 7

SPIRITUAL TEST

For as long as I can remember, I have always gone to church. I am not sure if my mom was pregnant with me while she attended church. However, she did attend church while she was pregnant with my sister. Spending time with my father on the weekends meant we attended church regularly. When I moved in with my father in 1994, church became a part of the normal routine. We attended church on Tuesdays, Thursdays, Sunday mornings, and Sunday nights. We had consecration service every weeknight in January for one hour. It was our way of preparing for the year when most churches held Watch Night Service on New Year's Eve. We had revivals, convocation, and 5th Sunday services throughout the year. We had prayer and tarrying services where we called on Jesus to obtain the Holy Ghost.

I was brought up in holiness. Most people associate holiness with Pentecostal, but holiness followed stricter guidelines. Women did not wear pants, jewelry or makeup. When women prayed, their heads had to be covered. We did not celebrate major holidays. We did not believe in sex before marriage or divorce. We were taught from the King James version of the Bible. I attended a small church with locations in Atlanta and Macon, Georgia. My grandfather was the pastor, which made my grandmother the first lady.

I officially stopped wearing pants in 1997. Besides pants making my skin feel like it was burning, I wanted to be obedient to God's word. Often asked in high school why I did not wear pants, it was always an interesting conversation. To keep it simple, I would say it was due to my beliefs. Most times, that would be sufficient. Other times, people wanted more details and Scriptures to support what I was saying. I learned quickly, some things are better left unsaid.

When I got old enough to make my own decisions, I was still unwavering in what I believed, the way I was raised, and the things I was taught. I was actively involved in church. I was a part of the choir, usher board, women fellowship committee, and finance committee. I learned very early, only what you do for Christ will stand. Therefore, I was intentional about doing what I could to please God. This was not always the case. Although, I did not go through a period of rebellion, I did go through a period of resentment. I was told I had to get married because I got pregnant with Alijah. Initially, I thought getting married was the best decision in the eyes of God. However, years later I learned He would have forgiven me for my sins and loved me whether I got married or not.

There were a few reasons I made the decision to get married. One reason was because I did not want to stand in front of my church to apologize for being pregnant out of wedlock. I remember a few of my cousins who had to do this, and it was very humiliating. I did not want to encounter this feeling. Another reason I decided to get married was because I did not want to lose the roles I held in the church. Any time someone got pregnant out of wedlock, they had to leave the choir until the child was one. She could no longer usher or hold any other positions in the church. Seeing others go through this made me not want to subject myself to the same. Therefore, I decided getting married was best.

Even though I got married shortly after I found out I was pregnant, I still had to stand before the church and apologize. Hurt, discouraged, and upset, I decided not to attend church. My grandfather sent a message to me from my grandmother or father that if I did not come to church to apologize, I would not be able to serve in my roles. I was still very angry, but I realized obedience was better than sacrifice. Even if I did not agree, I needed to be obedient to my grandfather's request. Therefore, one night when I returned to church, I got up and apologized to our congregation.

Feeling embarrassed by what I was forced to do, I was very mad with my grandparents. My grandmother was the individual who told me I had to get married because I was pregnant. Then my grandfather was the individual who told me I still had to apologize in front of the entire church. I just did not understand. I was perplexed. I was livid. After one of the most humiliating moments of my life, I stayed out of church for a few months. I needed time to process things. As a young adult, I was still living my life for my family. I was still concerned about what they thought. I was doing things to please them rather than doing what was best for me.

After speaking with one of my close friends, she made a valid point. She told me people are so caught up on religion instead of building a relationship with God. I sat there for a moment and reflected on her words. I liked the sound of building a relationship with God versus being so focused on religion. Religion was all I knew. I was taught about religion for many years. I do not recall a time where there was a strong emphasis on building a strong relationship with God.

After that conversation, I realized I wanted to build a relationship with God no matter what that looked like. First, I knew I had to return to the root cause of my hurt, frustration and resentment. One of the things that caused hurt, frustration, and resentment was being forced to get married. In addition, being required to stand in front of the church to apologize for getting pregnant was another reason I was upset. Being told one thing and having to do something else was not good. Nonetheless, I started attending church again, and I asked God to forgive me for anything I had done wrong. I was finally in a place where I could forgive my grandparents for their suggestions, advice, and demands about getting married. Even though it caused me to make the biggest mistake of my life, I could finally forgive and move forward.

One day while I was watching a movie, the characters delivered a very profound message. A mother was telling her daughter to forgive, not for the other person, but for herself. She indicated that if she did not forgive a person, they keep the power. That message resonated with me a lot. I do not want anyone to have power over me because I was too hurt to forgive. I feel confident in knowing that God will fight my battles. Therefore, I can forgive, let it go, and move forward. Besides, I loved the thought of having a close relationship with God. I did not want to do anything to impact that. I also did not want my inability to forgive to prevent me from receiving God's grace and mercy.

When I started focusing on building a meaningful relationship with God, I stopped being concerned about what others thought, how they felt, or what they had to say. I believed in my mind, if God be for me, who could be against me. For so long, I lived my life to please my family. I was finally at a place where I was living my life for me. I finally understood there was only one person who would judge me. I was intentional about building a closeness, stronger bond, and deeper relationship with God. I wanted the Lord to order my steps in every aspect of my life. I wanted to live a life pleasing to Him. When I turned 30 years old, I was finally in a space where the opinions of others did not matter. Although I did not want to let my family down, my biggest concern was letting God down. I did not want to let him down in any way. This new commitment to God allowed me to pray, fast and talk to him more. I built a relationship that was meaningful and impactful. I was no longer concerned with religion. Rather, I was focused on building a substantial relationship with God.

As I began this new relationship with God, I discovered the spiritual connection I had with him. God talked to me and showed me things directly or indirectly. Sometimes, I would see things, and other times God would use others to give me a message. For example, when my grandfather died in 2017, I left work to pick up Alijah from school. The initial route was taking longer than expected. At the very last minute, the Holy Spirit led me to turn around and take a different route. I was obedient. Even though I knew the new route would take me longer to get to the school, I knew it would avoid the traffic I was sitting in. As I got closer to the school, I noticed a slim, young male who resembled Alijah walking away from campus. I thought to myself, "I know this is not my child off campus when he is supposed to be at school." It *was* him. I wondered where he was going, what he was thinking, and why he was off campus? I was truly disappointed that I witnessed this. Then I was reminded, if I continued on my previous route, I would have arrived at the school later, which meant I would have missed seeing Alijah leaving campus. I would have arrived on campus attempting to check him out, for the school administrators to tell me they did not know where he was. The knots in my stomach tighten. I was upset. I was disappointed. I needed to know why Alijah felt it was okay to leave campus for any reason during the day. As I pulled into a parking space at the school, Alijah was coming across the parking lot. Extremely upset at this point, I asked, "What are you doing off campus?" He attempted to explain it was lunch time, and he was going to the store to buy a snack. I told him that was totally unacceptable. I asked him who gave him permission to go to the store, who knew he was gone, and what if something happened to him while he was off campus. I explained to him anything could happen, especially when he is supposed to be in school. I asked him, "What if I got to school to check you out and no one could find you because they did not know where you were?"

The thought of this created frustration, fear, and worry. I told Alijah I did not care if it was his lunch time. He was supposed to remain at school all day, from the time he got off the bus in the morning, until the time he boarded the bus in the afternoon. I remember telling him, "The school is responsible for you during the day. Therefore, if I come to the school and you cannot be found, my problem is going to be with the school administrators first."

When I finally calmed down, I realized God was in complete control. He needed me to see Alijah leaving school. Within the next few days, Alijah's band teacher confirmed he saw him leaving campus as well. I knew at that point this was not a one-time occurrence. It was meant for me to see Alijah leaving campus, so I was prepared for what was coming from his teachers. I talked to Alijah again about leaving school during the day. I explained that anything could happen to him, but most importantly no one would know because he was supposed to be at school. I did not know if I made sense to Alijah, but I prayed he would listen. That instance was the first of many where God showed me things directly or indirectly. He always talked to me.

Soon, Alijah wanted to know how I knew everything. I explained to him due to the relationship I have with God, he keeps me informed. Alijah did not believe me for a while, or he just did not care. Finally, after several instances of discovering what Alijah was doing, he was afraid. He asked me one day, "Mom, how did you know that? Wow, that is scary." Again, I shared with him that God shows me things and every time He wants me to know something, he tells me. This allowed Alijah to be a little more cautious in his actions, but not fully. He still tested my patience, and I had to rely on God to restore my peace. With the closeness I developed with God, came a deeper level of discernment. I was able to use spiritual guidance to help me view things clearly and critically. Not only did God show me things, but He talked to me as well. It is encouraging when you may not know how something will work out, but God already knows the plan He has for you.

I was concerned about covering some household bills due to unexpected car repairs. I needed my car to get back and forth to work. However, I did not want to cause my household bills to be late, because money was used to cover the repairs. I pondered for a little while about what to do. After a brief moment, the Holy Spirit said to me, "Reach out to your father." I was a bit hesitant, but I wanted to be obedient. Since my father was no longer working because he retired, I knew his income was limited. I did not want to cause any financial strains for him. After some time had passed, I finally called my father. I explained to him what was going on with the car and what needed to be done. I told him what the cost would be. I also told him I could cover a portion of the cost, but not in full. Once I provided all the pertinent details to my father, he simply asked, "Can we put it on a credit card?" I took a long pause and silently thanked God for making a way. Instead of paying the difference of what I could not pay, my father took care of the balance in full. I asked my service advisor if it would be feasible for my father to provide his card details over the phone or if he needed to present it in person. My service advisor confirmed it would be suitable to provide the details of the card over the phone. I was grateful. God is faithful through it all!

Another time God showed his faithfulness was when I was fasting and praying about finances. I was waiting for funds to become available but was unsure about when I would receive it. As I was cleaning the kitchen one afternoon, I heard the Holy Spirit say, "Check your account." A little anxious, I logged into my account. After checking my balance, the tears began to flow down my face. The money that I was told would not arrive for a few days, had already posted to my account. Overwhelmed with joy, I gave all praise to God for finding me worthy of his blessings. In that moment, I realized God would always make a way, even when I could not see a way.

One of my favorite Scriptures comes from Proverbs 3:5-6, 'Trust in the Lord with all thine heart; and lean not unto thine own understanding. In all thy ways acknowledge him, and he shall direct thy paths." God's grace and mercy have played an integral part in my life. When I find myself in a place of worry, fear or frustration, listening to gospel music always helps. There is always a message God speaks to me in those moments. Some of the words I hear in gospel music resonate with me so much. There is often an overwhelming feeling that comes over me. There is something about music that truly feeds my soul. When I am feeling down, tired, and consumed with things, I listen to my gospel playlist. Something so simple makes a difference in my life.

My father always encouraged me to give God some of my time. In an effort to do so, I found out just how beneficial it could be. The relationship I have developed with God over the years is very rewarding. That relationship gets stronger every day. By building a personal relationship with God, it allows me to pray and fast more. It causes me to connect with God on a deeper level. It helps me trust Him more. I finally realize God's timing is always perfect. I know things will not always work when I expect them to, but it will work out for my good in the end. It was necessary for me to develop a personal relationship with God. My family could only bring me to church. It was up to me to discover what a life with God was all about. When I stopped focusing on religion and developed a relationship, it allowed me to truly encounter the presence of God.

When DE and I discussed religion, he made it clear he was spiritual. It also meant he was not necessarily concerned about a certain religion over the other. It further proved we should develop a relationship with God instead of focusing so much on religion. For years, I shared with family and friends that my religion is holiness. Now I simply make it known I have established a strong relationship with God. When I need my peace restored, I know who to call on. When I have a difficult time, I know who to talk to. When I am dealing with pain or sickness, I know who can heal me. When I am too tired to pray, I know he hears my heart.

I made the decision to build a relationship with God because it was something I wanted to do. I was not forced to do so. For once, I wanted a spiritual connection that would serve me well in this lifetime. I learned a lot over the years from my grandfather's teaching. However, the personal experiences and encounters made the difference for me. Many have mixed feelings when it comes to believing in God or a higher power and attending church. I strongly suggest people encounter God for themselves. No one can impact your relationship with God, but you. I know from personal experience that once you have encountered the goodness of God, life will never be the same. I am grateful for the spiritual connection I have developed over the years.

Not only do I encourage myself to have a relationship with God, but I encourage my son as well. I challenge him to be an example and role model for the younger generation. I share with him some of the same words of encouragement my father shared with me. Alijah knows when he is not working, he should be in church. He has no complaints about going to church. He enjoys helping his grandfather by beating the drums and taking part in Sunday School. I remind him, only what he does for God will stand so he should do as much as he can, while he can. I am intentional about living a life that is pleasing to God. I understand my help comes from Him.

Chapter 7 Lesson

On this journey throughout life, it is necessary to develop a strong relationship with God. Often, we focus on religion instead of focusing on building a solid relationship with Him. Understanding where your help comes from through the storm is crucial. On our spiritual walk with God, we must understand yesterday is gone, tomorrow is not promised, so we must be intentional about cherishing each moment He blesses us with. Learn to live in the moment!

PERSEVERANCE

Chapter 8

CAREER TEST

I have always considered myself to be a hard worker. While attending high school, I always wanted to do my best because my grades were a direct reflection of me. When I entered the workforce, I had the same desire. I wanted to do my best because my performance was a direct reflection of me. On July 7, 1999, I started my first job in retail at Cato Fashions. Since I had no prior experience, I knew effective training would be vital. My store manager was very sweet, understanding and caring. She made sure I felt welcome and received adequate training. If I had questions, she made sure she was available to assist. Since a church member helped me get the job, she helped me with any questions I had as well. I worked very hard. I went to work on time each day. Sometimes I stayed late if coverage was needed.

Within six months, I was promoted to 2nd Assistant Store Manager. My store manager was preparing to move back to Florida which was a very sad time for us. Change is often difficult, especially when you get used to certain individuals. However, we knew the change was coming and the store had to be prepared. The store manager was responsible for making sure the store had a sufficient management staff before leaving. She felt I was the best individual for the job. As the youngest employee in the store, being a manager created some challenges. It was often said by store associates that I was too young to make decisions. I was told I was inexperienced. It did not matter to other associates or managers that I performed very well the first six months in my associate role. I was 18 years old, and most could not get past my age. The co-store manager who would be taking the store manager's position was not happy about the decision to make me a manager. She did not think I was ready. Some of the older employees did not like the idea of me leading them. It basically meant I could tell them what to do, when to do it, and how to do it.

The church member who helped me get the job was very proud of me. She encouraged me often. She told me to do my best and prove them wrong. I did just that. When I started in the 2nd assistant manager role, I was responsible for the accessory department. The accessory department included shoes, hats, scarfs, home good, sunglasses, jewelry, and anything that was not clothing. I was responsible for floor sets and displays. In addition to having an entire department to manage, I was also the person who opened or closed the store. Each morning, I had to take the deposit to the bank. Since I did not have a car, that meant another manager had to take me or two other associates had to go before lunch time. I was also responsible for training new associates, processing shipment, organizing, recovering, preparing for inventory, and submitting change orders. Things went well for a long time.

Then I started experiencing some challenges with my new store manager. We bumped heads often. She had an inability to talk to me with respect, and that bothered me. It was clear she did not like me. The reason she did not like me was unknown. She tolerated me because the previous store manager tried to convince her of the value I added to the team. Most days things went smoothly. Other days we bumped heads and I could not wait to leave. It was always something petty.

Working at Cato became extremely stressful. Thankfully, I was preparing to take maternity leave. It was almost time for Alijah to arrive. I was extremely grateful for the time off work because I needed a break. Sadly, maternity leave went by very quickly, and after just six short weeks, I returned to work. When I got back from maternity leave, I received another promotion. It was quite a surprise since the store manager did not like me. I discovered later the district manager encouraged the promotion. I was no longer the 2nd assistant manager. My new role was 1st assistant store manager. I had the same responsibilities, but I received a pay increase. With the promotion came more stress from the store manager. It seemed everything I did was wrong or not good enough. Any time a store needed a manager to fill in, I always volunteered. I capitalized on any opportunity to get out of my store. I knew my time was coming to an end. However, rather than leave, I stayed until the end.

One night while closing at my store, I allowed an associate to process a return for me. Not realizing this was an issue, the store manager discovered this and asked me several questions. It was clear she did not believe the information I provided. Therefore, she reported this situation to our district manager. I felt I had a good relationship with the district manager which meant this situation would be resolved quickly. However, when the district manager told me she needed to investigate and get back to me, I was confused. Why did this situation require an investigation? What rule did I violate? What did I do wrong? One of the worse experiences for me came when I worked all week for a company, not knowing if I would have a job at the end of the day.

I was filling in at a different location for the week. At the end of my shift on Friday, my district manager stopped by the store for a follow-up meeting. I was nervous. I did not know what to expect. My heart was beating fast. My hands were sweaty. My head was pounding. As soon as I sat down, the knots in my stomach got tighter. The district manager shared with me the return was considered fraudulent since I purchased the items, but had the associate return them. I explained we were the only associates left in the store. Therefore, I allowed the associate to process the return for me. Based on the investigation, I broke a rule. After five years with the company, I was released from my role as 1st assistant store manager. Even though I was unaware of the broken rule, there was no grace for me. Instead of giving me a final warning, the district manager decided to let me go. I was upset and frustrated. I felt the issue could have been resolved inside the store, but my store manager found it necessary to report it to the district manager. I never knew why she disliked me so much, but it had finally impacted my livelihood.

Shortly after leaving Cato, I was hired with Ross. I was hired on the spot at a job fair. The manager of the Stonecrest location hired me specifically for her store. She had a full-time role she wanted me to fill immediately. I got back to work shortly after being hired. My new store manager was very sweet, and she taught me a lot. Again, I was responsible for the accessory department. However, it was much bigger than my last store. There was a lot more to do and it included a fine jewelry department. Working the fine jewelry counter meant I was a key holder. This meant I had to be certified to do so. It was truly a humbling experience.

I soon learned there was some level of stress from working in any retail store. Ross had major visits from corporate executives often. In preparation for these visits, we had to work overnight. It was a bit overwhelming, but I was grateful to have a job. My job at Ross was not enough. Therefore, I started working as a cashier for Target. Since Ross was in Lithonia and Target was in East Point, I submitted a transfer request. The commute back and forth just did not make sense anymore. After only a few weeks, my transfer was approved.

I really enjoyed working at Target. A new opportunity became available working in the cash office. I was extremely excited when I was selected to fill that role. Working in the cash office was less stressful. It was quite enjoyable even though there was a lot of responsibilities that went into that role. When Ross discovered the skills I had working in the cash office, they wanted me to assist with their cash office as well. However, they did not have a full-time role available.

I eventually left Target and went to Staples full time as their cash office associate. I often worked two jobs at a time. It was necessary to stay on top of my bills each month. I was still young, so I was unaware of the toll the constant standing, walking, bending, and lifting was doing to my body. After about a year at Staples, I left for a better opportunity with Drive Time. Drive Time was the first office job I had. I truly enjoyed it. We worked Monday through Friday and rotated on Saturdays. It was more money, and I sat in an office all day. After a few years with Drive Time, I left and went back to Ross full time. When I returned to Ross, I was the front-end supervisor. This role was responsible for the front-end staff, training, developing, maintaining the front end, and assisting customers with purchases, returns, exchanges, or addressing concerns. It was another stressful role. However, I remained in that role because I needed a job with steady income. In 2009, I received an opportunity with Public Storage. I was grateful for another office job that I could sit versus stand all day. However, the role was not fulfilling. Therefore, after a few short years, I went back to Ross full time. I do not know why I stayed in retail so long. Maybe because it was my first job. Maybe because I performed so well. Maybe because it paid the bills which was most important. However, working in retail was starting to take a toll on my body physically and mentally.

One afternoon while assisting customers, I started having chest pains. I alerted my manager and sat down in a chair near the front door. The chest pains worsened. At some point, someone called the paramedics, and they took me to the emergency room. After the medical professionals ran a series of tests and checked my heart, they informed me that I had an anxiety attack. I was clueless. I had no idea what that meant. After further explanation, they asked me if I had been under stress lately. I knew exactly what the root cause of my stress was - Ross. Wow! I never imagined working for a company would impact my health. I had some tough decisions to make.

God showed me several times, in many ways, it was time to leave Ross. However, I kept holding on until I had no choice but to leave. In March 2013, after nine years with the company, they let me go. Even though I felt they discriminated against me, I was relieved because I was no longer with a company that did not know how to value good people.

Within just a few days, I had two new job offers. One was with Goodwill, another retail store. The second job was with Alora, a call center role making outbound calls to current customers who used phone, cable, or internet services in their homes. When I received a letter in the mail indicating I was approved for unemployment from Ross, I decided my time in retail had come to an end. Instead of accepting the job offers, I decided to focus on school while I received unemployment.

I realized it was time to find my passion. What did I want to do for the rest of my life? What was my overall goal? What was I good at? What could I do that would make the greatest impact? I knew I did not want to be in retail all my life. I started thinking about a career and what would make the greatest impact. Within a few weeks after leaving Ross, I started a tutoring business. My son was playing football and the parents knew I was in school. One evening while at practice, one parent asked, "Do you tutor?" My response was, "I do not tutor, but I can." Within a short time, I was tutoring different kids at the park. The parents were quite impressed with the improvements their children made. I was grateful for the positive impact I had on my kids. It was truly humbling. Within a few weeks, I had 10 kids that I tutored. The parents referred my services to other parents, which is the reason my business grew so quickly. Things with tutoring went well. However, sometimes things are not as consistent as we need them to be.

Unemployment was coming to an end sooner than later, and I needed additional income. Against my better judgment, I decided to explore opportunities in retail. After one successful job fair, I was hired on the spot with CVS Pharmacy. I tried to convince myself it would be different because it was not a clothing store, but in my heart I knew better. The only difference was there were not many clothes for purchase. The managers were the same, the customers presented the same challenges, and the hours were long and stressful.

One of the managers who interviewed me during the job fair was very kind, friendly and passionate. As it turned out, he was transferring to the store I was hired for as the store manager. I was excited. I thought based on his helpful and friendly demeanor during the hiring process he would be a great leader. I was totally wrong. He was arrogant, messy, and very unprofessional. I always speak up for myself when something is wrong. He did not like that. He was very rude and mean when communicating with me. He was also responsible for making the schedule which meant he controlled how many hours I worked. Working for CVS became just as stressful as it was working for Cato, Ross, and so many other retail stores. One day after work, the Holy Spirit reminded me, I was removed from retail for a reason. I promised myself when I left Ross, I would never return to retail again. Here I was in retail again because I knew I had the experience and knowledge to do the job. Often, fear causes us to go back to old things because we are comfortable there. When this happens, things become uncomfortable, and we are forced to make changes.

I did not work for CVS on Saturdays or Sundays. Therefore, when I left work on Fridays, I made sure I had my schedule for the following week. When I checked the schedule, the manager had me scheduled Monday through Wednesday from 6 a.m. – 2 p.m. When I arrived on Monday, I could not clock in. The message on the time clock indicated I was not on the schedule, so a manager override was needed. Confused, I walked to the back office to view my schedule. When I checked, my name had been completely removed from the schedule. Annoyed at this point, I walked to the front of the store to ask the store manager if I was supposed to work. He snapped at me by saying, "What does the schedule say?" Trying not to match his tone, I told him I was on the schedule when I left on the previous Friday and now, I was not. Therefore, I asked the question again, "Am I working today?" He told me to clock in and he would give me an override. At that point, I knew it was time to go. There was no reason for me to be taken off the schedule. Yet, I no longer had a schedule.

When I left CVS that day, I did not return to work. Hire Dynamics, a staffing agency I registered with for office jobs, called me for an interview with Gas South. The representative provided details for the interview which included date, time, location, and things to expect upon arrival. When I went for the interview, I gave it my all. I answered questions in a clear and concise manner. I gave a brief overview of my experience and education background. I shared with the interview panel why I would be a great fit for the job. In addition, I asked questions.

Initially, the representative from Hire Dynamics called me back with disappointing news. She mentioned I was not chosen as one of the 10 candidates selected, but I was number 11. A little down about the decision, I still pushed forward, nonetheless. The next day, I received a second call from Hire Dynamics. As it turned out, Gas South did want to offer me a job. I was so excited. When she told me, I started orientation the next day. I was so grateful.

Ironically, the same day a manager from CVS called to give me an update for my schedule. When she told me the store manager added me back to the schedule for the following week, I laughed. I shared with her that he should probably remove me from the schedule because I no longer worked for CVS. She was surprised, but she understood. The next day I went to CVS to provide the management staff a resignation letter which was effective immediately. Of course, the store manager was upset, but it did not matter. He was being messy by taking me off the schedule. I was not rude, disrespectful or unprofessional. Yet, he removed me from the schedule for no valid reason. Now, he had to find someone to replace me permanently.

I was content with my decision. I never should have gone back to retail, but we live and learn. On Thursday, August 14, 2014, I started training with Gas South as a customer care representative. Immediately, I was drawn to the training function. I could already visualize myself in a trainer role. The possibility of becoming a trainer was encouraging. Plus, the trainer indicated she could use an assistant. The trainer was efficient and helped us learn a lot. Being a professional student most of my adult life, I did well in training. We took quizzes after we completed different topics. The way we performed on those quizzes impacted what shift we would get when we finished training.

We were in training for five weeks. There were close to 30 agents when we started training. When it was time to go to the floor, we barely had 20 agents left. Agents were let go for various reasons: attendance issues, personal, and transportation challenges. There was even one agent who was terminated for sleeping in class. I was extremely grateful for the opportunity. Therefore, I made sure I got to work on time, participated in training, asked questions for clarity, and studied for quizzes.

When it was time to select our shifts, I was very nervous. I was not sure if I would get a late or early shift. During training, we worked 8 a.m. – 5 p.m. which was the ideal shift. However, there were other attractive options. The trainer made it clear that shifts would be based on performance during training. Since I did extremely well during training, I received my first preference which was 7 a.m. – 4 p.m. I was ecstatic. Not only was my new job outside of retail, but I received a great shift as well. I was so excited to embark on this new journey.

After a few short months of working for Gas South through the temp agency, I was offered a permanent position. This included a pay increase, medical, and dental insurance. Things were going so well. I caught on to my new job very quickly. If I had questions or concerns, I had strong support from my coach and team members.

Working for Gas South provided the financial stability I always wanted and needed. I was no longer stressed about not earning enough money to cover monthly expenses. The company also offered me overtime. We had contests which allowed us to earn extra cash. In addition, we received annual bonuses. Gas South quickly became a best place to work. I finally felt like I worked for a company that valued their employees. Not only did the company express their appreciation for us, but they proved it in their actions. We had several company-paid lunches, ice cream socials, special events, birthday celebrations, and gifts.

In January 2015, only five short months of being with Gas South, I moved into a new home and purchased a new car. I was truly blessed and grateful for the fresh opportunity God blessed me with. At the end of April, our fiscal year ended which meant it was annual review time. I had only been with the company for eight months, but long enough to be evaluated for my performance. When I met with my coach, she shared with me that I, as a new hire, performed better than some of the veteran agents. Once she went over my performance review, I discovered that I exceeded expectations in all areas. Based on this performance, I received special recognition and lunch with the senior team. I was extremely proud of my progress the first few months with Gas South. It was encouraging to do well and get recognized for it.

I soon learned that annual bonuses were very generous. Even though my bonus was prorated, due to my high performance, I still received close to $4,000. I was extremely happy and grateful. It allowed me to do things that I would not have been able to do if I did not get a bonus. Things were not perfect at Gas South. I experienced my share of challenges, but I made the best of it through it all. There were days when we were so busy, it was overwhelming. At times, things caused us to be stressed, especially when we had system issues. Other days, we had several meetings to attend or lots of training to complete. There was always something to do. There was a lot of changes to ensure processes were efficient and effective.

Shortly after starting with the company, the customer care department moved to the corporate office. That meant all employees would be in the same office together. This created a major shift in the culture. It felt good to meet individuals from other departments and feel like a family. The CEO was very personable. He took time to learn everyone by name. He also held meaningful conversations and created time to get to know us individually. It really made me feel good to work for someone who valued the team. It truly made a difference. After I completed a year with the company, I became eligible for additional incentives which included 401K match and tuition reimbursement. These incentives made the overall compensation package very attractive. I never worked for a company that provided 401K match or tuition reimbursement. Being reimbursed up to $5,250 every year was extremely helpful.

The culture, benefits, and additional incentives made Gas South a great place to work, however, the growth opportunities were very scarce. When positions came available, upper management already knew who they wanted to fill those roles. It was extremely frustrating applying for numerous jobs, but being told "No." For two years, I did not apply for any new job listed. A few opportunities became available that I could have applied for. In some cases, I was encouraged to apply, but decided not to. Finally, a communication role posted that I felt I was a great fit for. However, I was not selected for the position. Extremely discouraged, I decided I would not apply for any new roles.

I did not apply for any other positions until the Senior Management Team completed a reorganization for the customer care department. This meant positions were created, eliminated, and some were combined. If agents did not apply for a new role, their skills and pay did not change. If agents were selected for a new role, they received a pay increase plus a title change. I felt this was a great way to boost the morale among the customer care team. There were so many agents in the same role for years with no growth opportunities. The new alignment would allow agents to develop, grow, and perform other job functions.

The highest role in the care center was a specialist. This individual was responsible for taking supervisor calls, assisting agents with difficult calls, and training and developing agents. Since my passion was always to train and develop adults, I felt this was the perfect fit for me. I wondered if I truly had a fair chance obtaining a new role. I was not sure if I would be selected or not, but I had to try. If I were not selected, I could at least say I tried. After several interviews, the management team started announcing who got each position. Normally when someone within the company got a promotion, it was announced via email and posted on the company's intranet. When the care center received promotions, we did not receive the same announcement.

After five years with the company, I *finally* got a promotion to specialist. I moved from the lowest level in the care center, to the highest. God is good! He reminded me that "No" does not always mean no. It simply means "Not now." As a specialist with Gas South for the last few years, I have trained and developed several agents. I have collaborated with my peers to make processes better. I have worked on many projects to help enhance systems within the company. Training is still my passion. I look forward to the day when I have the opportunity to train agents on a daily basis for Gas South. I know when the right time comes, I will move into that role. For now, I will continue to walk in my purpose. Even if it is not with Gas South, I know God has major things in store for me.

Chapter 8 Lesson

Do not settle on a job because it guarantees a solid income. Yet, secure a role that will be meaningful and will positively impact your life. Discovering your passions and using those to make a difference in the world is key! We must leave a lasting impression on the world while we can.

Chapter 9

LETTING GO TEST

Have you ever been involved with a person longer than you should have? Have you ever worked for a company longer than you needed to? Have you ever remained committed to a relationship long after the expiration date? Have you attempted to make a friendship last after betrayal? Have you ever held on to someone or something that was no longer conducive to where God was leading you? I know at some point in our lives we can all admit to holding on to someone or something longer than we were supposed to. Why is it so difficult to let go? Why is it easier for us to settle or accept less than we deserve instead of walking away? Why is neglect, disrespect, physical, or mental abuse easily accepted? Why do we tolerate the bare minimum from significant others? Why is dishonesty, lack of intimacy, and insufficient affection so common among relationships?

I can admit I have remained in relationships longer than I needed to. I have also held on to jobs beyond the expiration date. Actually, it has been an ongoing struggle staying with a company that no longer valued me as an employee. Why do we struggle so much with simply letting go? For me, I held on to jobs because it was my security blanket. No matter how horrible the work conditions or treatment were, it still provided a consistent source of income. I knew I could rely on the company to pay me for hours worked every two weeks.

Having the reassurance that I could pay my bills caused me to remain in different positions beyond the expiration date. Often times, it took me losing the job or being forced to resign before I finally walked away.

I could not identify what I was dealing with during that time, but it was a clear sign of fear. There was a fear of starting over and finding a new job. I was afraid of losing my solid income. Even though the income never seemed to be enough, especially with the rising cost of living, I was afraid of not having it. Sometimes being in different roles caused stress and anxiety, but I still would not part ways.

In March 2013, after nine years working for Ross, I was terminated for making a purchase while on the clock. Sounds silly, right? Of course, it does. The store where I worked had recently gotten a new store manager. It was clear from the beginning she was not very fond of me. I was this young woman of color, with more knowledge, education, and experience than she had, but she was the store manager. I was simply the front-end supervisor. It was my responsibility to manage, train, and develop the front-end staff. She was tasked with running the entire store. I was always at work before my shift. I was always there long after my shift ended. I trained all the management staff to effectively process the cash office. Even after training was complete, I found myself still processing the cash office more often than upper management. I was always complimented on my professionalism. I was crossed trained in all areas of the store, so I was identified often as a major asset to the store. We always passed our secret shop. In addition, the front of the store was well maintained, and my front-end staff performed their jobs well.

When things were not going well, I verbalized my concerns to the store manager. I did not realize how much of a threat I was to her. It was not until I was sitting in the office with Loss Prevention trying to determine why I was being terminated. Supposedly, it was a rule that associates could not make purchases while on the clock. The purchase in question was made at the end of the night while the store was closed, and another associate checked me out which was the proper procedure. It was common for associates and managers to make purchases on their breaks or at the end of the night while the store was closed. I sat there thinking to myself, "Is this the best she could do to get rid of me?" It was in that moment I realized why that happened. When I endured my first panic attack months prior, I did not quit. When I was stressing so much about work that my weight was up and down, I still did not quit. After nine years with Ross, in a leadership role, my final pay was $9.89. Despite the obvious signs that it was time to part ways, I held on until God said no more. My time had come to an end. As the assistant store manager escorted me to the front, I walked out the store with my head held high. I recall telling the assistant store manager that "God makes no mistakes." Instead of being worried about no longer having an income, I was at peace. I was calm. I was happy. For the first time in such a long time, I felt a sigh of relief. When I got to my car, I promised myself and God that I would never stay with a company that no longer valued me as an employee. When I finally got home, I wondered what I would do next. I still had bills to pay. In addition, I had to take care of my son. After speaking to those closest to me, someone recommended I apply for new jobs and unemployment. I was more open to applying for new jobs instead of unemployment. I was always denied when I applied for unemployment in the past, so I decided not to bother. Instead, within a few days, I updated my resume and started applying for new jobs. At that point in my life, I had 14 years of retail management experience. It was basically all I knew.

Within a few days of being terminated, I had two job offers. One job was in retail as a store associate and the other job was in a call center. I had not decided which position I would take, but I had the job offers which was a great start for me. Once again, someone suggested I apply for unemployment. I was still very reluctant since I had no success in the past, but I applied. After completing all the paperwork, speaking with a Department of Labor specialist, and providing all necessary information, I waited for the decision letter in the mail. In the midst of waiting, I wrestled with which job I would accept. I wondered to myself which position would make the greatest impact on others, which would minimize stress, and which would provide financial stability. I was still undecided, but I was truly grateful I had options. Within a few days, I received a letter in the mail that indicated as a recipient of unemployment, I must attend monthly workshops. I was a bit confused because I had no record of being a recipient of unemployment. When I got back in the house, I logged into my account with the Department of Labor. To my surprise, I discovered I was approved for unemployment for up to 52 weeks. I was unfamiliar with how long an individual could receive unemployment benefits, but I was grateful I was approved. The very next day, I received the official letter in the mail with the approval for benefits. Not to mention, I discovered, I had a large deposit in my checking account from the previous weeks that I claimed benefits. It was such a tedious process, but it proved to work out in my favor. Instead of accepting the job offers I had, I declined both. I focused on taking care of Alijah, finishing school, and tutoring my kids. I was finally in a happy space, and I was grateful. I vowed in that moment that I would never return to retail. I felt God delivered me and there was no turning back.

Why does it take something so drastic to leave a company? This was the last time I remained with a company longer than the expiration date. The moment I realized Ross no longer considered me an asset to the company, was when I should have parted ways. However, I was concerned about no longer having my solid income. I realized God had never left me nor forsaken me in the past. Therefore, I knew he was not about to start. This experience gave me the strength to finally let go and let God. Instead of being worried about not having substantial income, my priority should have been my health and well-being. We live and we learn. This was truly a learning experience for me with a lot more room to grow.

As previously mentioned, not only do we hold on to jobs we should let go, but we hold on to relationships too. A relationship is not just limited to husband, wife, boyfriend, or girlfriend. It could also be mother, daughter, father, son, sister, brother, auntie, niece, uncle, nephew, grandparents, grandchildren, or best friends. When it is time to let go, it is important to do so.

When a relationship is causing more harm than good, it is time to release it and move on.

Experiences have taught me so much that I am mindful of things a lot sooner than I was years ago. For example, I started dating a guy in September 2017, which was only a few short months after my last relationship ended in June. When we met things were going really well. We spent time together, talked on the phone often, and we enjoyed getting to know one another. He traveled a lot for work, so strong communication was necessary if we stood a chance of building a happy and healthy relationship.

In December 2017, I started preparing for my company's anniversary party which is held each year in January. Since he and I were dating, I felt it would be a good idea to ask him to go with me. I was unsure of what his answer would be, but I was very happy when he agreed to go with me. We immediately started planning what we would wear, where we would eat, who would drive, and where we would meet. We were filled with so much excitement. I ordered my dress. I sent pictures to get his approval and he was impressed. He seemed to be just as excited about the party as I was. He even talked about going to buy something to wear so he could match my dress. I was looking forward to attending the party.

The week of the party he reached out and told me he could no longer attend. He told me his job opened an office in Tampa and he had to manage the office until a new manager was hired. Extremely disappointed, I accepted the fact that I would be attending my company's party alone. The day of the party, I reached out to him and there was no response. I called, but there was no answer. Not only was I now attending the party alone, but he was no longer responding to my calls or text messages. I was so bummed about him not being with me, I attended the party long enough to see close friends, take pictures, hear the announcements, and eat dinner. Not only was I annoyed that he was not there with me, but he was not communicating with me.

When I got home, I went straight to sleep. I thought when I woke up, I would have missed calls or texts, but there was still no communication from him. Days went by and weeks passed and there was still no word from him. I was extremely disappointed. There were so many things running through my mind. Is he okay? Did something happen? Did I say or do something wrong? Did he lose interest? What was the problem? I went from worried, concerned and frustrated to upset, pissed and annoyed. Why is simply communicating such a challenge for men? I could not understand, but I tried not to dwell on it. It was hard.

Days and weeks turned into a month. At this point, I was no longer concerned about where he was or what he was doing. I attempted to move on with my life. A few days later, I received a text that said, "I miss you." I was instantly annoyed and texted back, "You cannot be serious." Reluctant to hear anything he had to say, I allowed him to explain why it was almost 60 days since his last contact with me. He explained his job temporarily relocated him to Tampa and since he would not be in Atlanta, he decided it was best for him to cease all communication with me. I honestly did not understand his thought process, but I am known for giving people the benefit of the doubt. He reached out to me because he wanted to let me know he was coming back to Atlanta. I was excited but not impressed. He said he would see me when he got back to Atlanta.

Surprisingly, when he got back to Atlanta, he came over to see me. I had mixed emotions about seeing him. Something just did not feel right, but I could not figure it out. The fact that he did not attend my company's party was tough. Not communicating with me for almost two months did not sit well with me either. However, I continued to spend time with him to see how things would recover between us. He told me he would remain in Tampa for a few months but would come to Atlanta when he had the opportunity to do so.

Since he was going to be in Tampa for a few months, I decided to fly down for a weekend. He was very excited about me flying into town. I was happy to be getting away from Atlanta. A few days before my trip, he came into town. He assured me he would be returning to Tampa before I left Atlanta. That did not happen. Instead, he expected me to cancel my trip and stay in Atlanta since he had to work from the Atlanta office. Things were just not adding up.

I flew to Tampa and spent time with family when I arrived. It was good to see my uncles who showed me a good time and made sure I had the best food. He called to check on me, but I did not have much to say. I was pissed. Instead of running when I witnessed the first red flag or two, I decided to give him a chance. When I returned to Atlanta, I was expecting him to pick me up from the airport. After not being able to reach him, I took an Uber home instead. Extremely frustrated, when I got home, I went straight to sleep. I did not have much to say.

The next day, we had a big argument. It was the first time since we met that I experienced anger issues. Since I was a victim of domestic violence, there was no way I was going down that road again. Anything that looked like it could harm me, I cut ties with it immediately. Seeing that side of him allowed me to make the best decision for me. I told him it was best that we go our separate ways and that is what I did. Even when he called me, my decision had not changed. I knew he was no longer worth my time and energy. I was tired of wasting time that I could not get back. I was happy moving forward knowing I deserved so much more and would obtain more in due time.

Often, we hold on to things and people out of fear. We may be afraid of being alone. At one point, I had a fear of being alone. I quickly eliminated that fear. It is best to be alone, happy, and healthy, than in a relationship that is unhealthy and filled with misery. We may also be afraid of not having suitable income. Or we could be afraid of not being accepted by others. Even when we know these things are causing stress, pain, and anxiety, we continue to hold on. It is critical to have a spirit of discernment which simply means being able to judge well. When things are no longer aligned with God, it is time to let it go. Letting go does not mean you do not care. It means what you need matters more. Letting go is often necessary for growth, healing and restoration. Remember, doing what is best for you is priority over anything and anyone else. There is nothing wrong with starting over. Release it and let it go!

Chapter 9 Lesson

It is critical to have a spirit of discernment which simply means being able to judge well. When things are no longer conducive to where God is leading you, it is time to let it go. Letting go does not mean you do not care. It means what you need matters more. Letting go is often necessary for growth, healing and restoration. Remember, doing what is best for you is priority over anything and anyone else.

ACKNOWLEDGMENTS

First and foremost, I want to thank God for leading and guiding me during this journey. Thank you for ordering my steps and giving me the words to say. Thank you for your mercy and grace. Thank you for strength because without it, I could not make it.

To My King, David Encarnacion Jr. (DE), I love you. Thank you for loving me, encouraging me, and supporting me during this journey. Thank you for believing in me. Thank you for expressing just how much I make you proud often. Your love for me is refreshing, and I cannot convey how much I appreciate you. You are my rock, and I cannot imagine doing this thing called life without you. I look forward to forever together.

To Lisa King DeJesus, Thank you! There are just not enough words to convey just how much I genuinely appreciate your love, support, guidance, patience, meetings, video chats, transparent conversations, direction, and prayers. Thank you for encouraging, pushing, and motivating me from start to finish. I appreciate you taking on my project and making it a reality. I could not have done this without you. I am forever grateful to you.

To Ada Allen, Thank you so much! You have been an integral part of this journey and I cannot thank you enough. You encouraged me from day one, and I appreciate that so much. When I needed that extra push to get me through, you were right there. You made sure I did not get discouraged. When I did, you prayed for me.

PERSEVERANCE

You uplifted me. You inspired me in ways that allowed me to keep going. For that, I am forever grateful to you.

Meet Author Dr. Sheirra Marci

Sheirra Marci, born and raised in Atlanta, Georgia, always had a passion for writing. In 3rd grade, she created a story to satisfy an assignment for her chorus class. The director of music selected the best story to turn into a play which would be performed for the entire student body. Sheirra's story was selected, and that is where it all began.

Inspired by her English teacher in high school, Sheirra knew she wanted to write. In 12th grade, Sheirra won first place in the senior class writing contest. It was in that moment she realized she wanted to teach English because she loved to write. Not only was she passionate about writing, but she was very good at it.

In 2013, Sheirra obtained her first degree, from Atlanta Metropolitan State College, Associate of Arts in English. Shortly after in December 2014, she obtained her second degree from Kennesaw State University, a Bachelor of Arts in English. Determined to reach her goals, she enrolled in graduate school at Strayer University. In September 2017, she graduated with a Master of Education with a focus on training and development. Sheirra concluded her educational journey in June 2020 by obtaining her Doctor of Education with an emphasis on Adult Education from Capella University.

Her passion for writing fueled her decision to create *Marci's Creative Nspirations LLC,* which is a tutoring business serving students of all ages in reading, writing, vocabulary, test preparation, and basic math.

Perseverance: A Reflection of Pain, Passion, & Purpose is Sheirra's first published book. However, she is preparing for her second project where she expects to continue to make a positive impact on the lives of others. Sheirra reflects on her own personal experiences to encourage others to keep fighting no matter how hard things get and to never give up.

Sheirra is currently a member of The Bible Way Temple of God Church, with locations in Atlanta and Macon, Georgia. She is a member of the adult choir. She has one adult son, Alijah Sherrod Granville, who motivates her daily. Sheirra and her King, David, spend lots of time building their home renovation business, spend quality time together with family and friends, and travel.

Stay Connected with Dr. Sheirra Marci
Website: *www.authordrsheirramarci.com*
Email: *info@authordrsheirramarci.com*
Facebook: @DrSheirraMarciAuthor
Instagram: DrSheirraMarciAuthor40
Twitter: AuthorDrSheirra